RÉJEAN DUCHARME

THE DAUGHTER OF
CHRISTOPHER COLUMBUS

A NOVEL IN VERSE

TRANSLATED WITH AN AFTERWORD BY WILL BROWNING

GUERNICA

TORONTO·BUFFALO·LANCASTER (U.K.)

2000

Original title: *La Fille de Christophe Colomb*.
Originally published in 1969 by Éditions Gallimard.
Copyright © 1969, 2000 Éditions Gallimard.
Translation © 2000, by Will Browning and Guernica Editions Inc.

Antonio D'Alfonso, Editor.
Guernica Editions Inc.
P.O. Box 117, Station P, Toronto (ON), Canada M5S 2S6
2250 Military Road, Tonawanda, N.Y. 14150-6000 U.S.A.
Gazelle, Falcon House, Queen Square, Lancaster LA1 1RN U.K.
Typeset by Selina.
Printed in Canada.

Legal Deposit – Fourth Quarter
National Library of Canada
Library of Congress Catalog Card Number: 00-100951
Canadian Cataloguing in Publication Data
[Fille de Christophe Colomb. English]
The daughter of Christopher Columbus
(Prose series ; 44)
Translation of: La fille de Christophe Colomb.
ISBN 1-55071-106-7
I. Browning, Will. II. Title.
III. Title: Fille de Christophe Colomb. English. IV. Series.
PS8507.U4F513 2000 C841'.54 C00-900163-8
PQ3919.2.D78F513 2000

Contents

To the Young Man of Letters

Don't wait around for readers, critics and the Nobel Prize in order to
     consider yourself a genius, an immortal.
Consider yourself a genius, an immortal, right away.
Just think: if he waited, Henry Miller waited until he no longer had a
     single hair on his head.
Just think: if he waited, Albéric Cahuet waited for nothing.
Just think: if he's waiting, Jehan Ethiey-Blez,[1] who has nothing left of
     his hair but the roots, hasn't received any sign.
Go ahead! While there's still time, make the most of the life of a genius
     and an immortal.
When we're dead or almost dead, there's no more time to savor the life
     of a genius and an immortal.

To the Young Woman of Letters

If you are pretty and you feel lonely, my telephone number welcomes
     you with open arms.
If you are pretty and don't feel lonely, go to hell.
If you are ugly and you don't feel lonely, pray to God that it lasts.
If you are ugly and you feel lonely, go visit the electric chair salesman
     nearest you; apparently electric chairs are as good for suicide as
     they are for murder.

The Daughter of Christopher Columbus

On Manna, drunk, lying on her back on a soft bench,
A hen calls in her language for the head of the barber.
That provokes such a fuss among the tourists
That everyone almost drowns.

Farther on, taking her head in her wings,
The bird clucks, "Thief! Scoundrel!"
Through a keyhole she sees Judge Hooker
Exploding mattresses and cushions with dynamite,

Rushing to find the gold coins
Of his father – he too a big shot
Who got himself kicked once and for all by a prudish female bull.
"Hug me, my little one!" he had bucolically told her.

A certain Wen Wother passes by the fowl.
He's a toothpick architect.
With her versatile beak, the hen knocks him down
With a blow that only a gloveless boxer can give.

He faints. He gets up again. He follows the leghorn.
He's going to show her just what he's made of.
There are limits to the impudence of that crested hot-head!
He runs among the cars like a cricket among the flowers in a
    meadow.

Armed with two of those banderilla-like sticks
That he erects for a living,
He goes from trot to gallop, runs several red lights.
He's mad. He's had it. He's furious.

He's caught up with the crafty beast.
He jumps her, pokes her, pierces her, runs her through.
Lying in her own blood, she is like a crate of raspberries
Run over by a 100-wheeler truck.

II

A megalomaniac of minuscule size,
Going under a twelve-foot overpass,
Sticks his head out. A passerby, seeing him do it, yawns.
People always do as they are: that has always bored him.

Late in the afternoon of the twenty-fifth of this month,
This passerby is noticed by the other passersby.
He smokes his pipe by the wrong end;
He's put a sifter on his head and some flour around his neck.

This passerby, still the one who saw the megalomaniac,
Decides the next day to become mayor of Manna,
A square island cleared by Christopher Columbus
In the days when he still wore discoverer's boots.

On the great square of the aforementioned parish,
The passerby finds a hundred universities two thousand yards
      long.
Entering one of them, by way of greeting,
He sifts a little of his flour on the head of the rectum, a hairy one.

This university, like the other ninety-nine,
Like everyone on Manna and on Wother
(The neighboring island colonized by Wen's grandfather),
Wears black in mourning for the leghorn and is sad.

"That hen," says his host to the passerby,
"Had a heart of gold. You know, unless you are ignorant,

That a heart of gold is indeed worth its weight in gold. ·
Several have fought over that organ; all are dead,

Including our old mayor, Onemost Hinfamous.
If you want his job, you've got it. With all my soul,
I give it to you. No one on Manna wants to be mayor.
In order to be the master of this bordello, one must not be
    proud.

Pupil, professor and then rectum of this institution,
I have always been a steadfast admirer of that gallinacean.
Not more than a month ago, she would go from gable to gable
Denouncing the excesses of the barber, a strikebreaker."

III

The new leading citizen, Aristide Tit by name,
Is immediately christened Onemost Hinfamous
And proclaimed the spiritual son of his predecessor.
He's been smitten. He's all fired up.

At top speed, anxious to please,
He visits the big shots among his flock.
He goes to Judge Hooker, then to the notary,
An old man always in cahoots with the rabble.

"Christopher Columbus arrived here in nineteen hundred
    forty-nine,"
The latter tells him. "We still believed back then
That he had uncovered something new,
That he was the discoverer of North America.

Since his fall from grace,"
Pursues the notary, all the while eating his soup,
"Christopher lives alone, almost a suicide,
At the water's edge in a launch with his daughter."

IV

It's raining. It's blowing. It's thundering. There's lightning. It's
    ugly.
As on all the islands of the world,
On Manna, from time to time, the weather is bad.
In the water surrounding the archipelago, fish abound.

Columbia Columbus, daughter of Christopher Columbus, my
    dear girl,
Is slender and beautiful like a little bird.
Besides, born of the famous egg of her notorious father,
She nearly became one of those beings borne by the air.

In her large, black boots full of cloud-pee,
She walks on the river. There's something to intrigue you.
She fishes off the coast on foot. You can see her sitting
On the waves when she is tired.

When one is a good product of our civilization,
One fishes from a yacht or perhaps a trawler.
Daughter of a fallen father, poor and lacking connections,
She floats on her feet. It's a disability.

The sky sprinkles her like crazy and she fishes.
Her method is simple and laughable.
She has a bow and a quiver full of arrows;
When a fish comes up for air, she shoots.

Columbia is as thin as a toothpick.
A bottomless pit, Christopher gulps down all her fish.
Contenting herself with swallowing and re-swallowing her
    Adam's apple,
She watches him do his thing, hoping that he'll become less of a
    glutton

And will take on the habit of leaving her one little one.
Columbia isn't mad at her dad for leaving her nothing to eat.
Proud of her father, she says to herself, "What an appetite he has!"
She goes from cupboard to cupboard, putting away whatever
    there is to put away.

In their big launch equipped with a roof,
They love each other like two turtle-doves.
At night, he snores like a skunk.
Listening to him, she thinks that he snores like a bull.

V

Columbia is alone but she doesn't complain.
Besides, what use is it to whine?
After all, she isn't in such bad straits
With birds, fish, insects and mammals.

When she is not fishing, she walks around
Here and there, munching on a potato.
She studies with supreme indifference
What moves on the ground and what moves in the air.

She has her ambitions, her dreams.
She wants to become a funeral director.
Under her top hat, she will lead those who kick the bucket
To the land of total silence and complete darkness.

When a frightened bird
Leaves behind its worm and flies away,
She smiles sadly, face turned toward the sky,
Believing that the bird took her for a fool.
When she was little, demented people scared her.
When she was as defenseless as a swallow,
She fled lunatics as the otter flees the trapper.
Now, she's a grown-up young lady.

VI

She doesn't go to school. She's quite right.
She already knows all about the exploits of Christopher Columbus.
As for mathematics, she can count her fish.
She always has her hands full of them.

When she makes a miraculous catch,
She goes to market, she does business.
With her spare change, she buys a pea jacket
For Christopher and some sweets for herself.

Never, ever will she forget the night
When, for reasons that remain mysterious,
All the fish had gone to sleep
On the surface of the river, in a full breeze.

That night, without bending
Her half-oak, half-birch bow a single time,
She could have filled up, believe me,
Several trucks and a few sleighs.

But, quite content to have filled
Her hemp bag as big as a bed
By putting in two hundred of the stronger cod,
She left the other water-dwellers alone.

Neither will she forget the morning
When the bottom of her container was broken
And she lost the few miserable small fry
That she had caught in four hours.

VII

Upon the left-hand summit of the hill,
Over where the dead of Manna are buried,
Columbia is sitting and watching far below

The scuffling cows, gilded by the sun.

She's bored but doesn't know it.
She thinks that finding nothing marvelous
Is natural, that from now till her death,
She'll neither hear nor see anything better

Than what she's already heard and seen,
Than what she hears and sees at this moment.
Around Manna and Wother, rumor has it
That the leghorn hen was her mama.

After a race of peerless grace,
She catches up to a cow and, like a toreador,
She seizes her by the horns.
She speaks to her, looking at her with sad eyes.

"So why do you want to harm
The other cows? Tell me! Speak! I saw you.
Once again it's you who started it all!
I'll have you know that war and violence are blunders!"

After kissing a hundred times the shiny nose of the guilty one,
She returns to the heart of the tombstones.
For being able to count on such an affable shepherd for free,
The owner of the cows, Judge Hooker, who is only turned on

By gold, ought to rub his hands with glee.
He has never shown any gratitude.
All the villages are full of people like that,
So much so that life often seems meaningless.

Columbia does not suffer from this state of things.
In the spring, the calves run up to her
And hold a party for her in which each one offers

To lick her sweat, which is like the finest honey.

VIII

An inquiry by Judge Hooker has revealed
That the leghorn hen, in the throws of her agony,
Rallied her strength and went
To bring Christopher her all but exhausted heart.

One may thus affirm that it is she who laid the egg
That was the talk of the town under the name of Columbus's egg
And from which was born Columbia,
Unremunerated cattlewoman, just for the fun of it.

The thieves of Manna and of Wother spread the word:
"Columbus has the hen's heart!"
Avidly and meanly, they strip
The funny little house of the so-called discoverer

(From its keel-less bottom to the unremarkable stork
Who sleeps each night on the mast erected on its roof of sheet
    metal).
They find less than nothing. Even Jonathan Jaylebyrd, the
    master thief
in this instance, can't find a thing.

Sleeping the sleep of the just,
Christopher and Columbia let them be.
They let them tear apart their timeworn drawers.
They let them turn everything topsy-turvy.

Christopher and Columbia are of the noble race.
They are not of those whose rest
Can be troubled by vulgar burglars.
When they go beddy-bye, they go beddy-bye.

IX

On average, Christopher Columbus travels once a year.
This year, he's off to Wother to see a long-time friend,
An ex-sailor who was on the Niña when
From afar were sighted the coasts of... Haiti,

San Salvador or the Dominican Republic?
Christopher doesn't remember very well any more
Which of the Antilles Islands was seen first. Rotten luck!
There goes his memory! This is worthy of Corneille![2]

The ex-sailor is now a port employee.
Christopher entrusts him with the heart of gold
(Which, by way of disguise, is viscous like an eel and has the
        form of two ears),
So that he will pass it on to Christopher's daughter

At the moment of his death.
"Protect it well, old chum!" says Christopher.
"I don't want my daughter, grown old,
To be a catastrophe for society."

Peeping through the keyhole,
The ex-sailor's son overheard everything.
Tapping himself on the tummy, he vows
To become Columbia's husband. He has never seen her.
"I hereby solemnly swear that I shall not allow
A dowry of that character and caliber
To fall into the moneybags of another. Mama,
The richer you are, the freer you are!"

X

Here is Columbia asking her father
Why water, which can hold up a brick,

Can not support a little pebble, and gives way under a small stone.
"Dear Papa, don't you find that funny?"

Christopher answers that water
Can carry such weight and cannot carry such lightness
Because of the bundle
Full of moonbeams that an alien being

Has attached to the bottom of each stream
In the world and of each lake in the world.
"Dear Papa, can these bundles be found?"
"Lice eyelids flutter when thunder rumbles."

Right away, Columbia steals an underwater diver's suit
And starts looking for her river's bundle.
After two days, she finds it near a polyp.
She breaks its ties and swallows it. Believe me if you can!

Which takes away from that waterway the power to carry boats
And gives this power to Columbia.
Which means that all she'll have to do is put the launch on her back
When Christopher decides to move, out of despair.

Which means that on the water where Columbia fishes,
No one will be able to navigate from now on.
The smallest rowboat will sink like a spade.
Must I truly reveal to you these secrets?

XI

Paul Blablabla, after spending two years
In each of the one hundred universities of Manna,
Crosses the river (by plane) to show his mama,
Who was living on Wother under the name of Joanna,

The handsome diplomas printed in advance that he has
    accumulated.
But Joanna is no longer living on Wother. She is no longer
    living at all.
She is dead. Nearly a century has gone by
Since she committed suicide by hitting herself with a master key.

"Surprise! Surprise!" meows to Paul the beautiful cat
That sees him ringing at the door of the cradle of his youth.
Only rats live in the old house now.
His distress is beyond measure!

Paul Blablabla sheds all the tears of his spirit.
His parchments receive it all.
They are dripping like bibs, all to hell.
What caused him to do all those long years of studies,

Despite his disgust for studying?
He's not very handsome. His appearance alone
Would not have been enough to seduce the Gertrude
Of his dreams. Why did he cram for so long?

For those who haven't really understood,
It's necessary to express the idea of the thing in other words.
As ugly as a hunchback flea, he felt himself condemned
To spend his life without a woman, without a Manon Lescaut.[3]
He had heard tell that the well-educated ones
Are as popular with women as the good-looking ones,
So he decided to become – and he was dumb –
The most intellectually attractive man of them all.

XII

Columbia doesn't know that some fish are poisonous.
She believes that all fish are fit for consumption.
After killing, with one of her resinous wooden arrows,

A magnificent orange-colored tricholome[4] carrying slow-acting
    poison,

She hurries to take out the bones,
To slice it into little pieces
And cook it. "Soup's on!"
She cries, as happy as a vicious old maid

Who has just found a husband.
"Father, I'm serving you a new kind of fish.
Come and get it! Try it right away, my dear discoverer!
Tell me right away that you think it's good!"

Christopher thinks it's so tasty
That he refuses, for fear of remaining hungry,
To grant the prayer of Columbia, who'd like some
In order to taste just a bit, a tiny piece.

"It's delicious. It's excellent."
But Columbia, a priori,
Prefers the glowing look
(As if it had passed through the oil in which the fish cooked)

That she has caused in her father. He has seemed
So unhappy to her, despite her respect and her good will!
"My daughter, in three hundred years
Your father has never felt so spoiled!"

XIII

After seeing the face and the legs
Of our poor Columbia, Paul Blablabla
Decides to write her a poem full of iambic feet
And to buy her a ring with a flat diamond.

"Your eyes are beautiful like your yoni,

Which is beautiful like your cheeks beautiful like your fingers
(The word sex, the true poets have shunned it),
Which are beautiful like your teeth beautiful like you.

I don't smell very good but I'm affable.
O sheath of my sword, I love you!
I'm not sexy but I'm admirable:
I have overcome them all, the one hundred universities

Which sow knowledge from Manna.
It was while thinking of you that I learned my lessons.
I didn't know you but the thing that I wanted to end up at
Was located at the place where your legs come together.

I thank from the bottom of my heart the master's degrees and
        doctorates
That mean that you cannot refuse, without being ridiculed
By everyone, to take my arm,
To spread yourself out on my bed like Jesus on the cross."

Paul Blablabla mails off his poem
And he goes to buy an engagement ring
At the worst jeweler's in the world. "Combien est-ce que ça
        coûte?"[5]
And he pays, without haggling, cash on the fingernail.[6]

XIV

Christopher has taught Columbia to do
Everything she's told to without arguing.
"Come under the elm whose trunk is wrapped in iron.
I'll be there tomorrow, tomorrow afternoon."

As one goes to the drugstore, she goes to the meeting
Arranged by this Paul, sight unseen.
She salutes the horrible boy who, on his knees,

Smiles like a fool at her bare feet.

"I don't have any shoes, do I?"
"Who would dream of reproaching you for it?"
"It's because we are as poor as rats."
"Cupid, by his arrow, has touched me.

Haven't you read my letters, O ingenuous sheath?"
"I haven't read them all the way, sir.
Papa didn't recognize half of the words."
"Hmm!" cries he, shooting her a pernicious glance.

The other Paul, the son of the ex-mate of the Niña, alone,
Bursts from the branches, suddenly, abruptly, all at once.
"Let's see if you're as strong with your fists as you are with
    your mouth!"
Paul and Paul go at each other like wolves.

It is Paul who triumphs, who comes out the winner.
One wonders which is the Paul in question.
Is it the Paul more learned than Paul Ricœur,
Or the Paul having the thoughts of a thief?

Paul Blablabla, armed with all his education,
Polished off the other,
Who, all bloody, cries out, "You'll regret these actions!"
And, head down, he returns to Wother.

XV

"Papa! Is it true? Am I truly engaged?"
Cries Columbia, holding her hand equipped with a ring
Toward the bearded and pain-pierced face
Of her failing father. He's drinking his last Cinzano.

"What, my daughter? You have a rope around your neck, at
    your age?"
And Christopher passes away with the image
In his head of Columbia in a wedding gown
And the noises of a shocking party.

"Papa is dead. That's a change!"
Her thoughts are elsewhere. The last words
Of the self-styled discoverer have bitterly disappointed her.
She's engaged to that hideous beast!

He made her close her eyes,
And put that ring on her finger,
And kissed her nose and hair.
She didn't have time to do diddly squat.

No way out. He got you, the rat.
You just have to swallow the pill.
When you're old, when you've got hairs down there,
All kinds of evils flourish.

She's going to have to marry
That acne-filled misfit now!
Cry, my pretty. Weep and wail.
Their children will be so ugly!

And she doesn't understand half of what he says!
And he smells of decomposed fish, so rank!
And her father lies dead on this bed!
Ah! Truly, she hasn't any luck!

XVI

To please her, they place
A top hat on her head.
Giving in to her most earnest desire,

They have her lead the masquerade, the party

That carries Christopher to his resting place.
So that she has more the air of an undertaker,
Jonathan Jaylebyrd lends her the black gloves
That he uses to steal in the dark.

Everyone shakes her hand!
They're all so attentive today!
They tell her not to grieve,
That time passes, you'll forget!

There are women who hug her!
Judge Hooker's wife herself patted her arm!
The notary's wife tells her to pull up her nylons
And says that her slip is showing.

They empathize with such great zeal
That she almost wants to cry.
"Scum like you gets picked up with the trash,"
Says a garbage collector to her fiancé.

Why did her father advise her to avoid
Her fellow citizens? They're so nice!
"You could have combed your hair, my little beauty!"
Her future husband snaps severely.

XVII

Ever since the pope permitted priests
To marry, like everyone else on earth,
The village priest of Manna has had in his heart
A boarding-school boy's crush on Columbia.

That Paul Blablabla, that intellectual, that communist,
Just let him wait, he'll get his!

He'll see how hard you hit when Christ is on your side!
And he doesn't forget in his prayers that the virgin has a small
     estate.

Like all the interested parties, the priest knows inside and out
That, through the good offices of the ex-mate of the Niña,
She has inherited a big heart of gold.
He'll see what kind of stuff I'm made of!

No! The ex-vicar won't let the ex-student
Pick the most beautiful flower of the bed!
If he has to, he'll go consult one of the wisest fortunetellers.
More and more, in the soul of the apostle, emotions reign.

The association of gawky old gossips
Has decided to place Columbia in a family
While waiting for the wedding. The priest has sent
Word to the holy ladies of his desire to lodge the poor girl.

"Forty-nine of the fifty stories
Of my luxurious rectory are empty!
The other parishioners, sad to say,
Don't have enough room for another hungry mouth.

Spare the poor! Make the rich like me
Carry the weight of the unjustifiable misery of the world!
Make me the tutor of this child! If she cheats on God,
I will be the one who scolds her severely!"

And when a priest gets going, I assure you,
He talks up a storm, he goes to town!
It's normal, with that sermon that he has to murmur
Every Sunday. He hasn't a single week of vacation.

XVIII

She won't kill anymore to feed herself.
Fishing is killing: she just realized that.
She'll steal potatoes and will swallow them raw
After going to wash them in the washroom.

Little by little she gets used to her orphan's life.
She does nothing more often than before:
She sits for longer periods on the hill;
Nothing very difficult about that.

The club of old, fake, driveling women
Sends her a letter telling her to go live
With the esteemed priest while waiting for the ceremony
That will make of her a servant sheltered from solitude and
      from frost.

Columbia, in tears, makes confetti of the missive.
Then, taking the yacht on her back, she goes to hide
In the thickest part of the big olive forest.
The priest has told her in secret that she would sin
If she were to marry anyone but him.
Now, she also was told by reactionaries
That she will be excommunicated if she marries
A servant of the Holy Spirit, the Son and the Father.

That is why, not knowing what to do,
She has decided to flee, to disappear from Manna.
When it is a question of her being absolved,
She will go see the Wother priest, one of Joanna's brothers.

XIX

Although she is not yet fifteen years old,
Ever since it's been known that she received a hearty inheritance,
Columbia has had no fewer than sixty suitors,

Each one claiming that the other is a worse fornicator.

Their age varies between twelve and three hundred sixty years old.
She has some of every kind, of every species.
There's Paul, the former sailor's son (how impatient he is!),
And Paul, the one who believes himself too knowledgeable to
    go to Mass.

There's the village priest and the village beadle.
There's the one who cuts wood in winter
And who does nothing when it's hot.
There's Dagobert, who wears his trousers inside out.[7]

There's the one who has no more teeth in his
Mouth, no more ears on each side of his head,
And who thinks he's the fancy fellah
Who supposedly invented the recipe for béchamel sauce.

There are others, loads of others.
There are mountains, heaps and piles,
From abroad as well as from Manna and Wother.
There's the one who eats only sieves and screens.

Five of the suitors, moreover, are women.
Let us mention, for those who are not yet aware,
That the law has just granted these ladies permission
To marry one another. It's sickening!

It's excellent for fighting the threat of overpopulation.
That's what the authorities told themselves, probably.
Then there's the German who says that his house
Is covered with cabbage rinds…[8]

XX

Columbia throws the heart of the special fowl into the water.
She found it ugly, horrible, hideous and cumbersome.
Hearing the bubbles, the suitors, sobbing,
Take the train and the plane back home. Some of them stay,
    however.

Remaining are Paul the well-educated, the village priest and a
    movie actor
Who is neither a star nor in the limelight thanks to his age.
Let us pity him who was once loved by the public.
The birds fly. The fish swim.

The farther we go, the worse my verse.
But it's none of your darn business.
Mind your own bees' wax
That cleans even as it waxes. Bunch of has-beens!

Just what is meant by all these familiarities with the author?
Will you be done soon?
Am I going to be forced to treat you as readers,
To take out my big ruler and spank you?

Bunch of nit-pickers! Zipper-openers!
Who do you think I am, anyway? This is way out of line!
That's it! I can tell that I've had all I'm going to take!
Farvosilicum bibendum silly bug with just the right curves![9]

What? You've never seen a pornographer?
What rock have you been under? Wake up and smell the city,
    dammit!
You can't even tell a pornographer from a phonograph?
Wake up! We've got civilization now!

XXI

Having put on the sexiest of her dresses,
One not as pretty as the pope's,
Columbia is off to look for a reputable convent.
She won't find one any time soon. Scientists, who undermine

Everything, have discovered that it is not sanitary
To live alone with God in a cell,
And they have had all the convents of Africa demolished,
The convents of the four other continents, too, everywhere.

Poor Columbia walks on, with the yacht on her back
And her favorite calf in the crook of her arms.
Inexplicably, the farther she is from Manna,
The better she feels, the less nausea she has.

Arriving in Italy, despite the bad smell,
She fells completely free and happy.
She tosses the ring of her long-suffering engagement into a river,
As if it were her unhappiness.

And it is near a truly minuscule stream,
Small in comparison with the rivers of Russia,
That she calls a halt for the first time since her departure.
Oh, the smell of spaghetti!

On the surrounding hills,
Many olive trees twist and turn.
All the poets have had only love
For this country. She decides to try

To nourish herself there and to find once again the peace
That she lost when she lost her father.
Besides, Christopher Columbus was not Polish.
There are enough pianists and drinkers who are.

XXII

"I am the daughter of Christopho Colombo."
Poor girl! That's all she has to say
And the Italians, whether ugly or handsome,
Line up, form ranks, exclaim, "Sure you are!"

And start to laugh like crazy.
"So you must have a little picture
Of the great discoverer, or maybe a shred
Of his shoelaces, or else the handle of his vice..."

"On Manna and Wother, there were no photographers.
There wasn't even a grocery store. Imagine!
Papa would walk barefoot like a giraffe.
He no more had shoelaces on his feet than he did rings on his nose!

As for the vice of which you speak,
It only exists in your head!
What would Papa have done with a handsaw? Come on!
What do you take me for, a bear-brained fool?"

When she launches forth into vocabulary,
She often takes a wrong turn.
Even with guns and revolvers,
She could not convince those fly-by-nights.

Those people don't take anything seriously.
Better watch your Perse![10]
Anyone who has been a globe-trotter
Will tell you: don't get involved with foreigners.

XXIII

The town hall sends her statement upon statement.
She owes a hundred lira in water fees and real estate taxes.
If she does not pay, the word is

That her reputation will be sullied.

Columbia, half dead with fear and fright,
Looks for a way to pay off her debts.
To her, an account is a count and a lira, my goodness,
Is a lyre. In order to pay up, she will have to be dishonest.
Anyone who is flat broke can't pay without cheating.
Everyone knows that. Debtors don't have the right to strike.
Now once and for all, stop the clichés!
The pen of the poet must be brief and to the point.

To save her honor, she will have to steal and bait.
Her accounts won't wait: they accumulate!
She runs the risk of being marquis bait
Or that a king intervene – what a curule fate.[11]

Columbia goes to see all the musicians that she knows.
If they have lyres, she tells them, "Hands up,"
Seizes the instruments, and ties them around the neck of her
        baby calf,
A strange beast who eats all kinds of thing-a-majigs.

Breaking the store window of a big-time luthier,
She slips away all at once
With the thirty-three lyres she still needs. "Berthier!"
Exclaimed Napoleon, "You're nothing but a dirty
        neck-chopper!"[12]

XXIV

In prison, Columbia neither complains nor laments.
Who doesn't like to eat three square meals a day?
A lawyer has taken her on as a client.
She would gladly have done without that vulture.

Charge a lot: that's all they know how to do

In that profession of drawing-room preeners.
In any case, they are far from upright
And they grope all the girls' tits.

"Prisoner-makers, dear jurors,
I've just returned from Manna. The blond-haired one
That I have the honor of representing
Is indeed the daughter of the mapmaker Christopher Columbus.

I call, as a witness, Judge Hooker."
Columbia finds that the magistrate has gained weight.
His briefcase is carried by a young woman.
In that briefcase, numerous false

Official minutes have been well filed
Which will assure that Columbia will be acquitted,
Acquitted for the worst as well as for the best.
She'll have to leave behind her three square meals a day.

She'll never again see the rats
With which she communicated at night,
Before falling asleep on her slimy straw mattress.
What a bother! Never satisfied! What a pain in the ass!

XXV

Her teeth hurt like crazy.
She endures. She does not complain.
She watches the children coming out of school
And sees her grown-up calf throwing itself in their way.

The animal, without any warning whatsoever,
Eats up a little girl's sandals.
A fight ensues.
The aldermen with their crutches

Inflict grievous harm
Upon Columbia's sole comrade.
When she gets angry, she is brave.
She throws a bomb at the aldermen.
"Wicked aldermen! Wicked aldermen!
In your place I would be ashamed!"
The aldermen decide to go have some wine
With pepper and ice cream.

What Columbia has told them
Makes them want to get drunk.
But the tavern owner doesn't extend credit
To a bunch of old cripples up to their ears in debt.

The tavern owner extends credit
Only to those who are rich,
Only to those who have thick
Wallets and valets up the yin-yang.

XXVI

She tries to pull out her infected tooth
With an enormous crowbar.
She borrowed it from a scarecrow.
She gets nowhere for hours.

The tooth-puller told her that he would relieve her pain
If she paid or if she accepted to work
For him as housekeeper for three full years,
Three years plus the time that she will have spent not working.

Columbia goes back to see the old scoundrel
And tells him that if he'll pull her tooth
She'll do anything he wants.
He tells her, "O.K.!" He is quite content.

The first day, the dentist's wife makes her eat
The tail and ears of her calf, her only friend.
They killed it and had it cooked under the pretext that, rabid,
It supposedly ate nothing less than Capri Island.

The second day, the son of the household
Hits her on the head with an enormous club.
"She is so awful, the new maid, so ugly
When she sleeps!" he says, to excuse himself, to his chubby
     mother.

The third day, the brother's sister
Pokes her eyes out, for no reason, just for laughs.
After getting other eyes put in by a jeweler,
Columbia leaves Italy never to return.

XXVII

Having found, along the way,
A porcelain sink as good as new,
She's seeking to sell it, so that she can have
Her next meal. She's in Paris, on the Pont-Neuf.

She really doesn't have any luck.
No one wants to buy the knick-knack.
For at least three months, every household
In France has had its own sink.

But Columbia doesn't give up so easily.
"Ladies and Gentlemen, I've just come from America.
And there, everyone has two of them, if not more.
What would you do if, like Pilate, the iniquitous one,

You suddenly wanted to wash your hands twice?"
Having tried everything, she throws her potential sale into the
     water.

Just there, in the water, a few feet farther on,
Someone is trying in vain to re-float a big steamship.
"Gentlemen, I have the power to carry vessels.
Will you give me something to eat if I help you?"
"Go ahead, doll!" they say, to make fun of her, just for laughs.
A little later, she comes out of the river with the boat called
    Manfred

On her shoulders and gives them a wink.
Of course, they can't believe their eyes.
"The Seine is a coffin for this big boat;
In the Atlantic, it would be better off."

Columbia goes to put Manfred in the ocean
And comes back. For her salary she wants a mouthful of bread.
"We didn't promise you anything!" say the loafers.
The poor wanderer is hungrier and hungrier.

XXVIII

"Go see what's up in Germany! There's a surplus of
    sauerkraut!"
Booed as though she had assassinated Charles de Gaulle,
She pulls together her last ounce of energy and hits the road
    again.
Traveling like that on an empty stomach isn't funny.

In Punburg, home of the great Mozart…
I wonder whether I'll ever get to the end
Of this Gallic epic.[13] Let us proceed! The arts
Need someone to twist their necks.

In Gruelburg, birthplace of the great Wagner,
The daughter of Columbus has the surprise of a lifetime.
She nearly has a nervous breakdown:
She's face to face with Jaylebyrd, the thief.

"Good old Columbia!" "My old pal!"
"What're you doing here in West Germany?
You're as white as a sheet!"
"What do you expect! East is east and west is west!"

He tells her that he has a good hold-up planned.
"If you help me, you get one percent of the take."
She tells him to stop fooling around.
"Let's go to the street corner and start begging instead."

Unexpectedly, Jaylebyrd listens to reason.
They set up shop under a big street lamp.
With four hands they hold out the hat of the one who just left
    prison.
At the bottom of the hat, darkly, gleams a revolver.

XXIX

They go from town to town.
They're raking it in.
They do thousands of miles.
They walk side by side.

Falling asleep on an island,
They wake up in a port.
"What a life!" they say to each other.
It's enough to bore you to death.

You have to be a ship
To love effortlessly
The life of a ship
A little more than death.

You have to be a khedive[14]
To believe effortlessly
That a lucrative life is

Preferable to death.

Ask a crocodile
If he prefers
To his nest of mud
An endless, aimless, empty exile.

Walking ceaselessly,
Always on their feet,
They are filled with sorrow.
You have to be pretty crazy
To be a vagabond,
And pass through without ever
Finding a place good enough
To set your snares.[15]

XXX

They lie down next to each other
Without fooling around.
When it's a port, they lie down on a cutter.
When it's a field, they lie down to the cries

Of grasshoppers, toads, crickets…
When it's hot, they sleep uncovered.
When it's cultivated, they lie down in the furrows.
When it's the sea, they lie down with the starfish.

When it's up North, they wake up
Under several feet of immaculate snow.
When it rains, they are amazed.
Why not? They're not wearing any shoes.

Do I ask you why you are amazed?
Besides, I know. You are never amazed by anything.
You're a bunch of scumbags! Ash-holes!

What did you do on earth? "I smoked."

Saint Peter's going to peter out on you!
When do you ever happen to laugh?
Never! You laugh about as much as a stone!
Just my luck to come across a bunch of fakirs!

Never laughs! Never even says hello!
Wears tinted glasses to avoid seeing you!
Talks about nothing but politics and cars.
Loves black tulips! Wears black underwear!

XXXI

Lying down like hunting dogs, they sleep in Istanbul.
Like two seagulls, they sleep each one on top of a mast.
The masts belong to a boat exporting soap bubbles
For washing pale hearts and pasty eyes.

They wake up. Their backs are killing them.
They wipe their eyes. They have clear eyes.
They have tons of reasons to smile at one another.
I caress your soul, you flatter mine. That's how it's got to be.

On the sidewalks of Istanbul, hat in hand,
They compete with sellers of rag-tag images.
As in New York and Hamburg, they do swarms
Of male and female monkey business.

They go into a restaurant and sit down.
They're hungry. Their stomachs are wide open.
The one who asks what they desire is Chinese.
The one who makes the coffee is yellow. He's not green.

Indeed, everyone in the establishment is Chinese.

They say to each other that they would have done better to stay
     in China.
What good is it to walk across a whole continent
If it's to see what you saw in China?

I don't know if you see what I mean.
If Earth were covered with Chinese, Earth would be no longer;
Earth would be China and it wouldn't be so funny.
Those Orientals aren't even hairy.

XXXII

Singing at the stop of their lungs, they leave Constantinople.
"It's in Istanbul that Constantinople
It's in Istanbul that Constantinople
It's in Istanbul that Constantinople…"

That's just about enough of that.
As songs go, it's not very clever.
Talk about a stupid love song!
But it sounds good in the dry morning air.

Columbia wants to try to catch up with the sun
And grab it by the circumference in one leap
(Has anyone ever heard of such a kooky idea?)[16]
Before it's too high above the horizon.

"Let's stop it in order to make an endless day!"
"Look at you: who do you think you are – Joshua?"
"You've got wit! You're funny! You're subtle!
Let's hurry up! It's getting ready to go behind a cloud!"

Patient prince that he is, Jonathan Jaylebyrd is willing to play
     the game.
Oh how they run! They go faster than Peter Snell!
The farther they go, the cloudier the firmament becomes.

It starts to rain. They've worn out the soles of their feet for nothing.

They'll try again another morning.
And in a lifetime, there are plenty of mornings!
They walk in puddles of rain water, in the muck.
Mornings? Tons of them. No need to worry about that.

XXXIII

Speaking of Joshua, here they are having an adventure
Almost identical to that of the man called Jonah.
They fall into their whale while jumping from the top of a fence.
The stomach wall of their swallower is carpeted with aces,

Aces of hearts, of spades, of clubs and of diamonds.
Probably the last one to make the trip was Dostoyevsky's gambler.
Columbia shouts, "Zero! Zero! Zero! Zero!"
To test the echo. They could easily ski,

The whale's spleen being as fat as a mountain
And lined with saltpeter[17] as white as snow.
It's hot. They should wear nothing but loincloths.
The fish has swallowed a little of everything. They have arm
       chairs to sit on.

If there were jacks, queens and kings,
They could play whist or 500 rummy:
At the foot of the heart lies a card table. Goodness me,
There's not much to do in a whale. "Just a moment!"
Answers the operator when you ask
To speak to Brigitte Bardot or to Paul Misraki.
They start to look for dice, in order to play dice.
In a whale, everything's really big. You can pee there

Just as if you were at home. If they had known, they would have
       brought

Something useful for killing time.
Not having anything else to do, they sing, with muffled voices,
"Jonah, in the whale, used to say, 'I want to… ' "

XXXIV

When you've been baptized, it's hard
Not to spend eternity in heaven.
Al Capone showed his baptismal certificate without any qualms.
Saint Peter was like putty in his hands.

They made the mistake of leaving him his guns.
A few months later, he had organized a syndicate,
Overthrown God the Father, and made himself master of paradise.
Tipped off by the distilleries, the angels and saints call him papa.

Al needs a good croupier for the baccarat table
In a casino that he's just opened, a casino reserved
For guys like Hitler, Bonaparte, Pushkin and Marat.
To pull that off you have to get up early!

Looking down on Earth with a little telescope,
Al sees Jaylebyrd begging with a revolver in his hat.
In order to see better, he asks for a big telescope.
Saint Peter brings the object. That's the kind of guy he needs.

Al Capone can't get over it. He didn't think that, on Earth,
In nineteen hundred and sixty-five, there could still be
Guys with smarts, with know-how.
"Even a Ness couldn't catch that one!"

He speaks of Jon, of Jonathan Jaylebyrd, to all his buddies.
"That guy, it'd take four FBI agents
To collar him, to haul him away!"
Like all Italians, Al loves his mother and garlic.

XXXV

Columbia awakens in the iris-perfumed dew and clean couch grass
Like a new penny on a summer morning in Eastern Canada.
She was awakened by a certain Paul-Émile Ropre,
A dope. "My name is Paul-Émile. How're you doing?"

Since Columbia only speaks Russian, she can't answer him.
For those who haven't read closely: Manna is in Belarus.
Columbia sees a fat green chicken. It has just laid
An egg. Columbia eats it raw. She doesn't eat it fried.

But where in the world has her irreplaceable Jonathan Jaylebyrd
    gone?
She looks to the south and to the west. She looks to the east and
    to the north.
The ex-burglar is nowhere to be found. She feels quite strange.
In her stomach and her heart, she has something stuck, like
    daggers.

She searches through the whorehouses. She goes over all the
    hotels and motels
With a fine-toothed comb. The only human friend she has ever had
Has disappeared. She goes into a church and, on the altar,
She has votive candles lit. The Virgin Mary hasn't seen a thing.

"You are not telling me the truth, O Mother of the Crucified One.
You who went up to heaven on a bicycle, you can see everything.
Where is he? Where is he hiding? Where is he hiding now?"
Al Capone told Mary to shut her trap
If she didn't want him to end her cult.
He has always really liked to make her mad.

Taking the form of an eagle, following Jupiter's lead,
Al took Columbia's only friend by the shoulders,
Lifted him up and carried him off like a helicopter.

He tore him from the earth and brought him to a place far from
    the cat's meow.

XXXVI

Columbia feels lonely, twice as lonely as before
Recognizing Jaylebyrd in Gruelville.
"You're not alone when the wind is with you!"
She says to herself, trying to play a trick on her sadness.

She concentrates on feeling each movement of the breeze on her
    body.
She removes her clothing so that she won't lose a single puff of air.
She walks on without stopping, until she's worn out.
She falls asleep in a deep ditch full of shit.

She wakes up and starts walking again.
It's the one and only thing that she can do
Between lunch and supper, between meals.
There's not much to do on earth

For those who don't love glory more than string,
For those who aren't interested in politics.
When a Pomeranian sheepdog runs after her,
Barking and hankering to bite her, she takes off.

And when Columbia Columbus takes off,
There isn't a dog in the world that is capable
Of catching her. The hateful ones will ask,
"Why doesn't she participate in the Olympic Games?"

All at once, a vodka-exporting
Truck almost runs her down.
Farther on, the truck has a collision with a tractor
And explodes. Columbia makes the most of the situation by
    getting drunk.

XXXVII

But I have not told you the tragic end
Of the yacht in which Columbia enjoyed,
By way of her father and her hunger,
A reason for living as good as those

That are sold at crazy prices
In all the department stores.
I'm opening a parenthesis? That's what you think!
I'm no more afraid of Sardine than of Shark!

Having had her eyes gouged out by the dentist's daughter,
She had become almost completely blind.
When one can't see, one can only tell an organist
From a Spanish cow by its bellows.

To go to the eye-setting jeweler's office,
She took the old yacht on her back.
Along the way, which she only knew halfway, at best,
She never stopped tripping. The fado

Is Amalia Rodriguez's specialty.
Columbia constantly fell on the ground,
Lost her footing, hurt herself and fell head over heels.
Suddenly, she found herself between heaven and earth:

She had just passed over the ramp of a bridge.
Columbia, as we know, knows how to swim. She swam.
As for the yacht, as we know, it had no bottom.
It lost its life. It sank and drowned.

XXXVIII

Poor Columbia almost died. Suddenly,
After wandering without meeting a familiar face
For a period of at least one year,

She comes face to face with the skinny stork

Who, in the good old days, every night,
Used to come sleep standing up on the yacht's mast.
How happy she is! How sweet is a friendly look!
She is so excited that she sees everything as if through a
        magnifying glass!

"I'll follow you, wherever you may go!" squawks the old wader.
"Of course, only if you want.
Going to Rome, to Marseille (but I don't want to impose),
I think is more interesting as a twosome."

Columbia takes one of the bird's quite wrinkled feet
Into her hands, and covers it with kisses as she cries.
After which she takes a pair of scissors
And cuts the thread of her tears. She still has some illusions!

She cries once in a while, she does, after all!
In the faces one meets on the street,
There are only cynical sores and bitter pustules.
Guitar-strumming singers say that men stink.

With an aged, astonished, delighted stork
On her head, Columbia tries to find something unknown
Along a road that she's traveled a thousand times.
Her motto is: "There's some left, so keep going."

XXXIX

Columbia and the stork avoid the asphalt
And the telephone poles that line it.
They walk through woods and through potato fields.
They advance among woodpeckers, porcupines and anemones.

To make her travelling companion laugh,

The ancient wader has put on her head a megaphone
That she found rusted in a swamp.
These objects resemble funnels, my goodness!

They suddenly see, between two giant maples,
A large like-new yellow Cadillac,
As surprising as a house in the middle of an ocean.
Behind the wheel, rear end up, is a widow.

This woman, whose husband died, is dead as a doorknob.
She has earthworms all up her nose and in her ears.
You all know that rot has a strong odor.
They bury her, taking care to let her toenails stick out.

Columbia doesn't know how to make an automobile obey.
The stork, who has had a wealth of experience in life,
Knows how. But, being without hands as well as eyelashes,
She could not drive even if she were dying to.

The stork squawks to Columbia how to set about it.
"Now, press lightly on the accelerator!"
The tires crush some lilies. Tires sure aren't tender.
You learn fast when you have a stork as instructor.

XXXX

Columbia's hair is so fine and so blond
That, sometimes, the stork pecks away at it.
For flying fowl, what's beautiful seems good to eat,
What delights the eye ought to delight the tooth.

With the Cadillac, their hobby is not stamp-collecting,
Their hobby is collecting speeding tickets.
Those of Kuwait are not like those of the United States.
Long live the difference! Their hobby has them hobbled.

As for the infamous gasoline,
They get it where they can, obviously.
At a hundred miles an hour, the stork looks ill:
She yells at her as a mistress would her lover.

"Too fast! This isn't the Indianapolis 500!"
Like all old beings, she can't stand speed.
"Turtles never get stopped by the police!"
Columbia thinks only of the speeding tickets. O, youth!

When they ride under the ocean or under the sea,
They close the windows of all four doors,
Quite carefully, all the way up,
So that the salt water won't ruin everything.
Sometimes, they capture a cloud with a lasso
And put the vehicle on it as one would on a barge.
Before tying themselves to such a vessel,
They bring together a good supply of acorns.

XXXXI

A tire goes round and round, then it splits.
You know how it is…
All the Cadillac's tires, whitewalls,
Explode at once. What a noise it makes!

Right in the middle of the road, like a millipede
That might have had all its legs cut off at the thigh,
The Deluxe can no longer move. Like a potato,
It remains motionless on the road, a mile from Nice.

But they are not short on resources.
Indeed, a spectacular tractor-trailer comes along just then.
But what are they going to do to make it stop?
They trip it up with a good Italian move.

Stunned, upside down, the big truck puts up no defenses.
It lets them unscrew four of its thirty wheels.
"We could replace the motor, might as well."
They undo the straps on the truck's motor.

Over time, some of the Cadillac's headlights have grown weak.
The truck has a hundred perfect ones, one of every color.
They don't hesitate. They go right ahead. Welcome to El Dorado!
They spend hours on the changes and the repairs.

Why, instead of working so much,
Didn't they, quite simply, take possession of the truck?
That question is so stupid that we shall have it stuffed with straw.
In El Dorado, people mind their own business.

XXXXII

Columbia and the stork cross through Greece.
In Greece there are Greek men and Greek women.
Being a good Catholic, Columbia goes to Mass.
In May, in Greece, the air is dry.

Since, legally speaking, the stork has no soul,
She is not obligated to go to church every Sunday.
In Greece, there are cripples and people who are blind in one eye.
The stork squawks, "To be frank,

I'm just as glad not to be required to attend all
That transubstantiation stuff."
"You jealous atheist! You ought to go hide!
To make fun of you, I'm going to call you Sister-tend-all."

Greece is a little bit like Italy.
There are many men, women and cats.
Men and women there sleep in beds.
Cats put on airs of pashas.

All along the Adriatic, it's rocky.
The Adriatic is nothing but a tranquil little sea,
Just a little stretch of commonplace blue water,
Nothing but very ordinary, when all is said and done.

When she wants to go see Greece underwater,
Sister-tend-all only has to flutter her wings a bit.
Pardon me if I have disturbed you.
Have you been to see the latest Buñuel?

XXXXIII

In Yugoslavia, there reigns an epidemic of all kinds of thefts.
The capital of that country is Belgrade.
Who is the head blocker-of-dancing-in-the-round? Tito.
There is a mean little town called Belle Glade

In the heart of Florida, which hangs like a sock
Off the southeast corner of the United States. In Yugoslavia,
There are some who are disgusted with Tito. They call him
    Tick-Tock.
There are others who are quite happy with him.

Columbia and Sister-tend-all get their Cadillac stolen.
Naturally! And by a pickpocket, to top it off!
"Goddam mutha-fuckin' sons-a-bitches!"[18]
Columbia curses in Huron when she's really angry.

With a fever of 104° Fahrenheit, a stork dies.
Ever since they must, as before, walk,
Sister-tend-all has had a temperature and has been crying.
And not a single veterinarian will treat her without cash!

Sister-tend-all is going to pass away. This is it! She's croaking!
When I hear France Gall[19] sing in false Yankee,
Shivers of fright run up and down my spine. O, French lips,

What or who will save us from our own slang?

Chattering to herself like a fool, Columbia leaves
The State where she lost one or two friends.
She does nothing more and nothing less than bite and scratch
	the ground
Dampened by her tears, while screaming, "Miserable country!"

XXXXIV

In Bulgaria, dear friend, everything is different, unique.
Human beings there have tails, and wagtails
Have shitloads of problems. Columbia travels as though in a clinic,
In this country that no more has a capital than it does a county seat.

Everywhere, my angel, the government governs alone.
Everywhere, it's three-thirty or four-fifteen.
Here, my girl, the government is the only thing governed.
Here, it's thirty-three never and zero's dead.

Everywhere else, the clocks are in the houses.
Here, my weasel, the houses are in the clocks.
Everywhere, men only fish and bring in the harvest.
Here, and may no God depart from this beautiful rule,

They also make the wheat and the fish.
In other countries, only the dishonest have guts.
Here, my sister, only the crooked-fingered eat the thief's bread.
Here, my child, the generals are the only ones who march in rows

Of shallots. The others stagger along like revelers.
I sense that you don't believe me at all. What to do?
I sense that soon you're going to call me a liar.
Here, the one who tells a lunatic to keep quiet is a liar.

Columbia goes into the most chic restaurant in Sofia.

They don't want to serve her the coffee she ordered.
"Why?" "You don't seem poor enough." That's it!
And here, even the words are well ordered.

XXXXV

Columbia is in the country where
The largest of all African drawers is located.
This country is not exactly Kenya.
A drop of water is not exactly spherical.

You'll ask me what difference
There is between *the largest of all drawers*
And *the largest drawer*. I believe in my opinion that I think
That concerning that, I have no idea to offer.

It is dark on the Dark Continent.
There's reason for it to be, because for quite a while
The sun has been set. It is evening
And Columbia, her eyes, teeth and hair glowing

In the moonlight, pursues, no! *makes* her way.
In her heart, boredom twists and turns like an eel.
For fear of getting lost, she holds a few souvenirs in her hands.
In order to avoid being eaten by an owl, a caterpillar

Has come to hide in her nose with its roof-like slopes.
It has fallen asleep. Columbia was able to hear it curling itself up.
The silence is enormous. At her feet, a star falls.
Strung onto a rhizome, it would make a nice necklace.

The darkness, as thick as water, makes her feet heavy.
A little later, tomorrow morning toward five o'clock,
The parakeets and parrots will be awake.
"Columbia! Columbia!" they will cry in chorus.

XXXXVI

"Miss," says the interviewer to her,
"You are the one-hundred-ten-thousandth person
To cross the Pasternak-of-the-Seven-Pains Bridge.
I am inclined to guess that that astonishes you.

How do you feel? It is quite an honor,
Isn't it, to be interviewed by none other than I,
Who am the son of the one who lent his name to this cantilever
And who wasted away around ten months ago

At the respectable age of ninety-five.
How do you feel? A little dizzy?
I talk on and on…! My mouth is all bloody from it.
You seem quite embarrassed. What am I saying:

You truly feel awkward! You can't take any more!
There's certainly reason enough, young ladies and gentlemen!
Dear television viewers, this long-awaited report
Is brought to you by Screw Wee Corkscrews.

Without further delay, let's get back to the subject.
Dear prize-winner, are you not filled with emotion?
Button up your dress, I can see your tits.
For twenty-two years, twenty-two, the Bering

Strait has been spanned by this beautiful hyphen.
I'm telling you: you shall have one hundred and ten thousand krill
If you answer this question correctly:
How long has this bridge existed?"

"Twenty-two years!" answers Columbia without hesitating.
"You are victorious! You've won!
Here are the krill! You really deserve them!"
The krill is Russia's new currency.

XXXXVII

With the krill, Columbia lives it up in Moscow.
She rents an entire floor of the Hotel Stalin.
She eats tons of caviar garnished with sole eyes.
She tells them that she is the dowager of Sakhalin Island.

At the highest of the Haute Couture shops,
She has dresses sewn for herself in hard syrup.
Jos Bonhomme, exiled from Haiti, was the locksmith there
Of a descendant of Toussaint Louverture.

Through him, Columbia, by way of jewelry, has flatirons made
Of almonds, sugar, chocolate and marmalade.
The fact that she always seems like a dessert
Guarantees her popularity. Astronauts are lovesick over her.

When she goes into a theater, always late,
Everyone gets down on all fours and bends over backwards for her.
They recount her latest prank in every scandal sheet:
She bought a Picasso, put it on her hearth,

Sprinkled it with a high-octane gasoline and,
As if it were nothing unusual, set fire to it.
She lights cigarettes with bananas made of
Crushed dollar bills. "Wha' d'ya want?"

She asks the Nobel Prize winner come to shake her hand.
Since he's a Nobel Prize winner who's almost a hundred,
And Columbia will be twenty years old next winter,
Everyone bursts out laughing. They're rolling in the aisles.

XXXXVIII

Meanwhile, the true dowager of Sakhalin,
In her New York tenement, near Chicago,
Is washing dishes and making meals.

She has revealed her identity to a so-called Ostrogoth

Who is her neighbor and who reads the news every day.
"The dowager of Sakhalin…"Gadzooks!…
"Accused of killing one of her one thousand faithful lovers…"
The worn out man doesn't believe his old glasses.

Like all the United Statesians, his dream is to become
A millionaire. Right away, he asks her awful highness
To become his wife. She accepts. "So that our future
Will be assured, my wizened old woman, let us call in the press
      at once."

The latter arrives. "The true dowager of Sakhalin is here.
She's the one. The decrepit one who washes dishes.
Your competition has offered me a million for her biography."
"Sir, if that biography is dirty, if it

Deals without shame and without embarrassment with her
      nightlife,
We'll give you two million for it, without delay.
Let's not forget that contemporary readers read in bed.
Now, in a bed, what is interesting is not the price of onions,

But the posterior." The so-called Ostrogoth assures the press
That the biography is daring, unhealthy, ultra-intimate,
That all it talks about is thighs and buns.
The potential buyers turn over the promised sum, without
      compunction.

XXXXIX

The young sugar cane tamer who,
Ever since she's had no more krill,
Pays Columbia's hotel and whisky,
Has a most difficult nature.

Our heroine has had it up to here
With his bizarre and preposterous habits.
He's constantly putting out his cigarettes on his tongue.
The worst thing is that he removes his clothing

Whenever he meets an archbishop.
"Why do you do that?" she asks him.
With clenched fists and a dry look,
He answers while machine-gunning a trash can

That he thinks that if, in order to salute the least of women,
One agrees to take off one's hat, or whatever is on one's head,
Then in order to produce the same effect on a marquis of souls,
One should not rebel at the idea of a strip-tease.

"All the more so because their soutane is a skirt!
Really, my dear, where is the harm in it?"
It is useless for her to quibble.
His character is getting dirtier and dirtier.

The day before yesterday, to give you an example,
It was Tuesday, and he went to Mass.
"I see that you know nothing about temples!
Jesus Christ sacrifices himself every morning, impious
    dowager!"

XXXXX

As for those who make dishonest proposals to her,
They are legion. But Columbia is more aware
Of the facts of life than at the time of Blablabla and the seven
    hundred
Suitors attracted by the goods born of her mama.

She knows what the men who are nice to her
Are out to get. And she does not let herself get confused.

Let them do it with other people, their mortal sins!
She's not one of those lambs who lets herself be shorn.

She has seen, in the majesty and serenity of the cathedrals,
That Capone wishes her to remain pure. And so she shall.
No man is handsome enough to get her to harm herself.
Her victories are easy: Al does it all for her.

Having lived in the world, she understands that her boredom
Is benign next to the anguish of the majority of the others.
"Thank you, my friends. Thanks, pals. Your venom,
You can keep it. *I* am from Manna and Wother!"

They have to get up early in the morning and stick together
If they want to turn her into a jaded, blasé type like them.
She is tired of glamour. Long live the absence of happiness!
In that department, what she's just been through takes the cake.

Walking in the muck and the puddles
Without ever stopping, without anything to hope for,
Is not so funny; it's no river of gold.
What's even worse, you've got to be ready for anything.

XXXXXI

"Let's go see Manna!" she says to herself.
Columbia knows all the shortcuts.
She opts for going as the crow flies.
The longest road is that of the taxis.

She finds her homeland all burned to a cinder.
She falls on the ground, crying out and shedding tears.
"I see you again, sheath! Here you are again, Dulcinea!"
Shouts Paul Blablabla, coming out of his torpor.

Paul Blablabla has not lost

His talent for well-turned phrases.
"Oh! Are you hungry? Oh! Have you eaten?
I have a plump chicken on the end of my spear."

He leads her into a grotto
That is cold, humid and poorly lit.
She is crying like an idiot.
She is more than upset.

He can cuddle her at his leisure:
She feels too much sorrow to react.
She is totally out of it.
She should not have come back.

On the table where he has spread her out,
She seems all dislocated.
"You must be so beautiful in the nude!"
She does not have the strength to be shocked.

XXXXXII

Manna has not really fallen victim to a disaster.
In order to trick the insurance companies,
The island-dwellers, at the suggestion of Hooker, now a
    government minister,
Have simply turned the island upside down. Long live France!

They have put the island wrong side up, like a canoe.
The part of the island that was in the air
Is now under the waves.
They didn't lack know-how.

Taking all the cinders from their chimneys,
They spread them over what would become the surface of the
    island.
"Help! Fire!" They sounded the alarm.

Cries were uttered by the thousands.

The insurance companies believed and paid.
Manna, which now lives underwater, yes, underwater,
Is rich. The Mannese did not drown.
They asked the lake fish and the sperm whales

How to make do and they told them.
They live underwater, feet up, church steeples down.
The farmer sells his radishes head down.
The truck farmer sells his rutabagas on the waves.

The island, now, is sort of keel up.
If you don't believe me, go see for yourself.
With all your doubting, you'll make me have a nervous
    breakdown.
The thurifer[20] waves his whatchamacallit in the waves.

XXXXXIII

Why don't the little fish drown in the water?
Because in the water there is nothing that can cause them to drown.
Why do the little Mannese breathe well in the water?
Because it's as if they have taken away from the water its liquid
    aspect.

Long live tits! But their poor pants
Can't stay pressed for a minute.
But their little shirts and their little skirts
Can't stay starched at all.

Those among the Mannese who were dropsical
Don't seem dropsical at all anymore.
Those among the Mannese who cry when it's tragic
Don't see tears rolling down their cheeks in torrents anymore.

It is well-known that in the beautiful country of Bulgaria
Men and women have tails.
On Manna, a small island in Belarus,
Everyone has been aquatic for a year.

Tables and chairs are made of iron.
Everyone knows that those made of wood float.
It was necessary to destroy or else put the finishing touches on
A lot of things. Into the scatterbrains,

They put some ballast.
I must also tell you
That under the waves there's no phallast,[21]
No empty open vases, no rain and no fair weather (friends).

XXXXXIV

The apocalyptic vision that Columbia has had
Has made her sicker than a woman with cancer.
When she groans, Blablabla sweeps in like a whirlwind.
He is of the opinion that she has foot-and-mouth disease.

Once again, his learning leads him to err.
The more he cares for her, the sicker she gets.
She has become so thin
That even the most somber of hell's inhabitants

Would take pity on her.
The cold and the humidity of the grotto
Have more effect on the little road runner
Than all the remedies that are simmering

In Paul Blablabla's kettles.
The over-diploma-ed one not being originally from Manna,
The Mannese, being very nationalistic, did not
Permit him to come share their life under the waves.

The aldermen and the churchwardens of Wother
Having chased him out of his homeland by hitting him with this
        and that,
Because of an affair of which one speaks only in hushed tones,
He has had to inhabit one of the caverns as big as hoop nets

Of which the new surface of Manna is full.
With her head on a stone, Columbia is lying on the table.
Paul Blablabla, downily, is lying on the bed.
That ex-university guy is truly hateful!

XXXXXV

"You know, my beautiful girdle-girl, Manna is not really burned
        up…"
Paul Blablabla had only to say that for Columbia
To start her cure, to start getting better.
Paul Blablabla is disappointed. He is crestfallen.

He had observed the evolution of her illness while laughing.
He had believed himself to be watching the beginning of her
        cadaver.
"Dead, you would let yourself be undressed, cute little receptacle!
Your stomach, my beautiful mug, I could finally flatter it

With all the vivacity and impatience that I have for it.
Your thin ears, I could lick them as much as I like!"
Alone with this maniac, she spent a horrible year.
But the nightmare is almost over. She can stand up,

Take ten steps without keeling over.
Alas, she is still so weak that she
Has as much trouble opening her eyes and chewing her gum
As a weight lifter does catching a swallow.

"Pretty girls of your type are quite a bit nicer

When they're finished, when they've kicked the bucket.
Being a great scientist, I have a right to girls.
And I take them where I can find them:

Most often in cemeteries!
All of the living chick-clits that I know don't let me
Delight in my rights. They fight back. They defend themselves."
"Be quiet, I beg you. Don't say things like that!"

XXXXXVI
Now Columbia can go outside for fresh air
And daylight without feeling too faint.
Her host is still seeking to please her.
He disgusts her. He makes her puke.

He hides behind a broad stump
In order to watch her pee. That's nothing. Listen.
"When you're asleep and a mean little fly
Walks around clip-clop on your immaculate face,

I enter the fly in spirit and it's as if I too
Were going from the grass so sweet of your brow so blond
To the ever-so-slightly flared nostrils of your almost-Chinese
       nose,
Up to the hidden red summit of one of your tits."

He shoves similar obscenities in her face
Twelve hours a day and twelve hours a night.
O, meager Columbia, your chaste ears!
She has only her horror to defend herself.

She tries to get him to understand
That he is sick, that he is prize game
For an insane asylum. He won't hear of it.
He says that he is no more crazy than the Barber of Seville.

She tries to make him see the marvelous nature
Of the teachings of Christ and the apostles.
"Lift up your skirt a bit, I'll see better."
It goes in one ear and out the other.

XXXXXVII

"I thank you for everything that you've done for me."
He doesn't want her to go. He's crying.
But her bags are packed. This outburst of emotion
Troubles her greatly but she has no change of heart.

He takes out a big revolver and threatens her.
He has studied for absolutely nothing.
He realizes that education is only a farce,
That it no more impresses a woman than it does a dog.

He has been treated ignominiously
By things, by men, by himself.
He has nothing to lose. To kill or not to kill,
It's all the same to an unloved guy.

But his interlocutor doesn't want to die.
Forcefully, she throws a suitcase at him.
Hit in the heart, he's about to faint.
She is so afraid that she is white as a sheet.

She grabs the triggered weapon and places it
Between the sole of her foot and the bottom of a shoe
That she's seen hanging around under the bed.
She imagines arm-cutters, foot-piercers.

What is hidden there, on the edge of the path?
Is it a human being who cannot stop himself
From eating the ears of other human beings?
Columbia feels the need to hurry along.

XXXXXVIII

"Which people have been nice to me
Without wanting to hurt me in return?"
She thinks of her father. His stomach was king.
All he thought about was getting heavier.

Perhaps there was Jonathan Jaylebyrd.
But he left her like a thief: during the night!
God has done things badly. It would be a lot funnier
If in each being he had put the heart of a stork.

All at once, Columbia thinks again about Italy,
About the jail cell they were perhaps right to throw her into.
For having gotten her out of prison, did she even say thanks
To neo-Secretary Hooker? She must be rotten to the core.

She calls herself heartless and turns right around.
She thinks that she has not known more true friends
Because she has lacked appreciation. Did she not fail to show any
With Hooker, that unjustly ugly judge?

She's going to show him just what good feelings are!
In her steps grow trees of firm purpose:
Their branches are laden with the weight of blood-red mea culpa.
Five thousand regrets precede her in the form of toads.

If he likes appreciation as much as he likes money,
He'll be content, he won't be unhappy!
If the gratitude whose weight slows her down
Were water, you could float the kingdom of God on it.

XXXXXIX

She knocks with all her strength at the magistrate's door.
She knocks really hard because they're having a ball inside.
She knocks and knocks with one fist and then the other.

No one hears her at all, because of the music and the people
      laughing.

"Come on, guys! Come see this! What a joke!"
Before she's had time to say boo, they hoist her up
On their shoulders, loads and loads of dancers
Bouncing her like a ball from floor to ceiling.

One of them sets her blond mane on fire.
Another kicks her in the rear over and over.
A guy who claims to be Napoleon's nephew
Pours several glasses of beer in her eyes.

"It was about time you got here, pretty little wench!
We were starting to get bored to death!"
They blindfold her and put
Little poisonous snakes in her pores.

By dint of pure courage, she manages to extinguish the fire.
They get insulted. They set fire to her skirt, to her petticoat,
After pulling out strand by strand her magnificent hair,
Of course. They spit on her as Japan

Spat on the U.S. in nineteen hundred...
Forty-one. How funny! How they laugh!
They poke holes in her calves to suck her blood.
What is she supposed to do? She endures and she prays.

XXXXXX

They fasten her to the floor with long nails.
"It's Christopher Columbus's daughter! Let's hang her!"
They think she's dead. That won't change anything.
They detach her. They're worse than Paul Blablabla.

They set up a scaffolding. "Let's live it up!

Life is so short and the atomic bomb so close!"
A toast to all kinds, to the big mushroom cloud, to dessert!
Do you want some? Here it is! Happy is he who grabs

A little phrase with a nuclear flavor,
For he's sure to make friends among the young,
To get applauded by the effervescent scouts
And by the pubescent emulators of the high-society ladies.

"Don't hang her by her neck right away!
We want suspense! Suspense! Suspense!"
They hang her by one foot, then by the other. They play around.
They're young. They have to have fun. Pop psychology says

You shouldn't hold back. They don't hold back.
Let's do what the masterminds say to do!
Let's pee on the ground. Let's poop everywhere.
Me? Have complexes? I slammed my Grandmother

On the head with a flatiron!
Bald, Columbia is burning, Columbia is hanging on by a thread.
Two disheveled men take out her blackened tits and suck them.
Be like the Marquis de Sade. Believe me, it's great!

XXXXXXI

Columbia thinks of the revolver...
She takes it out. She cocks it.
She's blinded by blood and anger.
"Who's going to get blown away first?"

A deadly silence falls.
With two shots from the revolver, she breaks
Her bonds. They flee in a panic.
They are no longer such joyous revelers.

No longer quite the gay charmers.
Awakened by the silence, Judge Hooker
Comes out of his bedroom in his underwear,
Gazelle-skin boxers.

"Well!" he cries, all smiles.
"The daughter of Christopher Columbus!"
He doesn't think she looks so nice
With her lead-spraying weapon.

She tells him that it is he
Whom she has come to see. "Right this way!"
She follows him into his little office.
"Did you just arrive?"

"I have come to give you some appreciation."
As she says this, she bows, humbly.
From her bodice, consumed to the point of indecency,
Falls an avalanche of rubies, diamonds and aquamarines.

XXXXXXII

Bowled over, Hooker invites her to spend the rest of the night
In the pink room, the VIP room.
Flattered as can be, Columbia can only accept.
"In this bed have slept bank officers and monarchs."

Laughing, Columbia slips under the covers, forgetting everything.
Like Jesus Christ, she pardons her executioners.
The mattress is filled with owl feathers.
It's the first time she's ever slept on such a soft bed.

Actually, it's the first time she's ever slept on a real bed,
On something designed with the sole purpose of being a bed.
Grass is not designed with the sole purpose of being a bed.
Nor was the sand at the bottom of the yacht any more of a bed.

For such a marvelous thing to happen to her,
She just had to show a little appreciation.
On the pink walls are hung a hundred stuffed thrushes.
Two stuffed owls stand on the credenza.

Such fine, white sheets! Such soft pillows!
Four pink Corinthian pillars hold up the bed's canopy.
So many Venetian mirrors. She sees herself out of focus.
A couple of crucified bears in a painting by Dalí.

When you're really happy, you feel like dancing.
She stands up and starts spinning like a top.
She stops. She hasn't washed herself. She has ruined the sheet.
She has left a big stain. Ashamed, she ends up sleeping under
        the bed.

XXXXXXIII

When she was dowager of Sakhalin Island,
She didn't used to sleep in a veritable bed,
But rather in what was supposed to have been Lenin's
        wheelbarrow.
When she was an all-purpose maid for the dentist in Italy,

She didn't sleep in a real bed.
She slept in an empty matchbox.
It was a very big one. You had understood that.
Despite all these difficulties, she has no wrinkles.

She slept on soft straw full of pus
When she was in prison.
She has never slept in a thing that was one hundred percent bed.
If you still aren't convinced, that's just too bad.
I'm not in favor of paying you to believe me.
Besides, I don't have one red cent, not even a kopeck.

Columbia's desperation is immense!
She is as dirty as the bread in her cell

Was dry. "Ah! I am garbage!
I am a disgrace to humanity!"
In the darkness, she finds an enormous pitcher
Full of an excellent white wine from the Somme.

In the reasonable hope of finding a temporary way
To forget her failure, she drinks some of that liquid.
She drinks wildly, until she can drink no more.
"Death to discoverers!" she cries. "Death to the dauntless!"

XXXXXXIV

There is Manna-Water and Manna-Land now.
Of the latter, Paul Blablabla is known as the founder
For the simple reason that he was the first inhabitant.
He's as proud of that as others are of a scooter.

Tonight Judge Hooker was elected mayor of Manna-Water.
The honors and the powers all go to one and the same.
Before going to bed, he took some Eno smelling salts.
As for his wife, she patted her face with some kind of cream.

I know, I know! These details interest no one.
I know, I know! It won't stop the war in Vietnam
And the fact that no one answers the telephone at Miss
          Johnson's house!
Do you know the wonderful story of Flim-Flam?

He died in the song that we used to sing
Around the campfires, in the days when I suffered from diarrhea.
"Who will be in mourning, Flim-Flam Boom-Boom?" Boobs!
"Who will be in mourning? It will be the parish priest."

How happy one is between three and twelve years old!
Flim-Flam was "all black, his face all covered..."
When you're little, you throw pebbles at beggars.
I will tell you at length about the time that I pillaged

A whole field of tomatoes seventy acres across.
When I was little, I was a helluva rascal.
Today, in my mouth and my heart, everything is bitter.
As the English say: my goose is cooked.

XXXXXXV

"My girl," says Hooker, "spend at least a week here!"
Columbia, to be like everyone else, drinks coffee
With one little finger in the air and the other on an eyebrow.
"They wanted you hanged, a kind of auto-da-fé,

Because they were under the influence of heroin.
You must pardon them; boys will be boys!
Besides, your endurance has made you a heroine.
Stay here for a week! Show us some good will, some audacity!"

Columbia does not answer because her mouth
Is full of food and, in those conditions,
It is not polite to speak. She doesn't have much education,
But the little she has she uses. She has taken a shower.

She feels secure. Having, all in one gulp, swallowed everything,
She says to the judge that it is a pleasure to accept his invitation.
She wants to make friends. She won't let anything stop her.
She's fed up with feeling all alone like a fish

In a plate made of Kaolin porcelain.
She's had it up to her neck, up to her ears.
The mayor's house is full of human beings!
"If there is only one friend among the girls and boys

Who are on this property and elsewhere,
I will be content, I'll simply die of happiness."
As for the sheet that she stained, it has regained its whiteness.
She washed it for three hours. Her guilt remains.

XXXXXXVI

Judge Hooker has been to see his jeweler.
The rubies, the diamonds and the aquamarines
Fallen from Columbia's torso have brought him
The wherewithal to buy a thousand hit-men.

The longer he succeeds in keeping Columbia,
The richer he will get. Her gratitude
Will perhaps permit him to buy the bombs
That he has dreamed of since the tender age of two.

It's the one who is the most atomic
Who is top dog, who is king of the kill.
He dreams of becoming that more than does Bob Plastick,
The President of the United States of Outer England.

All he needs is a hundred other similar surprises
Stirring between the tits of that idiotic imbecile,
And he will be able to break Japan like a bottle.
The magistrate has been plotting for a long time.

He knows full well that if he could season
Those no-good Nippons with atomic bombs,
Everyone would be afraid – that the mere sight of his nose
Would take the wind out of their sails.

Adolf Hooker is not one of those effeminate types
Who stop along the way to listen to the flowers smell good.
He's a *macho!* He has big ideas.

He has a heart in his gut and nowhere else!

XXXXXXVII

Columbia turns off the lamp and shuts her eyes.
Once again the day is done.
At night, when you're tired, there's nothing better.
At night, when you're tired, it's a fruit

You savor, you chew on, your mouth closed.
Abruptly, the door opens. Suddenly, someone enters.
Her revolver is under her pillow. Better to be armed
When, as in this case, you can suddenly find yourself in the
    middle

Of the vehicle that carries souls back to heaven.
Who is that yellow shape approaching softly?
The subject has two bumps: it must be female.
The bumps are small: she must be thirteen years old.

It's the youngest of the voracious mayor's brats.
Columbia doesn't have much interest in girls.
She finds them false. They are superficial.
La-di-dah is what they are. They only like what glitters.

"What are you doing here?" she asks her.
"I'm here in my own house, in my father's castle.
I don't have to answer to you, turtledove!"
What does she have to thunder about? Who does she think she
    is, Thunder?

Suddenly, Columbia is ashamed of her misogynistic feelings.
What if, by scorning women, she should deny herself
    friendship?
She won't stick out her tongue at her, won't thumb her nose at
    her.

She'll give herself the chance to make friends with her.

XXXXXXVIII

"Your face is deadly serene. Is this from insolence
Or because you don't know that bitterness is in style?
I'm asking out of politeness – yeah, right!
You've missed the boat. Get going! You're far behind!

You're always grinning from ear to ear
And what is *in* is Juliette Greco's pout.
You don't seem to be with it, old girl.
You've got to look like you've puked all day to be beautiful
    nowadays.

Look like one of those sword-swallowers!
You must go to bed the wrong way round with the first guy who
    happens by.
When the last shout rang out, where had you gone?
You've got to have dead eyes. No clear eyes allowed.

I've come to see you in order to warn you.
If you don't change, you'll be laughed at by everybody.
Have a disgusted air. From now on, be grossed out.
If someone says 'Hello' to you, answer: 'Another one who is
    scared stiff...'

Society has an inside and an outside.
Whoever says 'Hello!' is insanely frightened of the outside.
Whoever says 'Hello!' wants to stagnate, to stay
Caught within. And that is ugly; it's nauseating.

Don't be taken for one of Panurge's sheep.
You must be taken for one of Godard's parakeets.
Shit on the bourgeois! Hurry up! It's urgent!
Just suffer! Esso's imperialism is after you!"

XXXXXXIX[22]

"Tell me your name," says Columbia, believing she's done the
        right thing.
"Call me Electric Razor! Those who call me
Jane, Mary or Rose, I tell them to go get screwed,
I skin them alive, I hit them hard with a shovel!"

"I'll do anything you want, Electric Razor.
I'll even confide to you my greatest secret.
I'm looking for friends, authentic friends,
Equipped with a heart and with the desires of a goldfinch."

"You make me yawn! In the genre, by the way, you are worse
        than
Classical airs, than the so-called great music.
Musicians are merchants of notes, salespeople.
And being of the happy customer genre is not chic."

The philosophette takes off all of her clothes
And lies down, so that her feet are on the pillow.
"So why do you lie down the wrong way round?"
"It's necessary, in all things, to explore the exterior. Do you
        want to try?"

"What does that mean? That I end up falling on my head?"
"That means and signifies that I like it when someone bites me.
Do you get it? Have you understood, Christopher Columbus?"
"Columbia Columbus, and let me tell you that you are wrong

To take me for a bear-brained fool,
That you are wrong not to try to be nice to me.
You reject friendship without knowing what it's made of.
Your empty soul could be full of joy."

XXXXXXX

Columbia is walking with Electric Razor in the woods.
Of all those who revolve around the judge while revolting,
The latter is the only one who is not
Entirely rotten: purulent outside, stale inside.

"Friendship, my dear Electric Razor,
Is the best there is in human beings."
"What's the best there is in Mexico?
It's the mines of gold, silver and tin."

Between the maples, salmon fly by.
Columbia's reddish orange eyes excite
The well-developed little girl. They drive her crazy.
"You can boast. I've been taken, seduced.

I wanna do it! That doesn't happen often!
Which means that I go for it when I'm psyched.
In a word: what I want, I take.
Give yourself to me, for I'll have you or kill you."

Electric Razor's eyes are quite odd.
"You can't take me, I'm married."
They pass under an immense willow.
On the virgin's ring finger, something has shone brightly.

A little pale, she grabs Columbia's ring finger.
On the finger, suddenly, a minuscule rainbow has taken shape.
"Do you now believe that I am married to God, Al,
That I belong to the boss of the one who was nailed to a cross?"

XXXXXXXI

"So, you go to bed with the Holy Trinity...
Your red eyes make my head spin."
"Those are not real eyes. A jeweler
Put them in for me. If they stink, I'm sorry."

Electric Razor uses a magnifying glass
To look at the mechanical organs of the hapless believer.
She grimaces like someone whose soup
Is too hot. Such infirmities enchant her.

For want of anything better, Columbia is afraid and takes pity.
What to do, Jesus? What to do, Virgin Mary?
"Christopher Columbus, I don't want your friendship,
But rather what the wife gives to the husband.

If you don't come to my room tonight
To turn over the goods, you'll regret it.
I have sixty rays with amber eyes,
And they are meaner than rats.

I have seven hundred high-voltage rays.
If you don't want me to sic them on you,
If you don't want to be electrocuted, behave.
Come at midnight; you don't have any choice."

Columbia weeps, then weeps some more.
Pierced by a thousand swords, her heart is pounding.
Who made this child so cruel?
Who caused her to act like the infamous Sade?

XXXXXXXII

God the Father, Al to his buddies,
Is the one who made a miracle
Take place around the victim's finger.

But more than a supernatural spectacle is necessary

To flabbergast an Electric Razor.
Al needs virgins for his celestial brothels.
He doesn't have enough left, goddammit!
What a pain in the neck, immortal clients!

Almost all the female saints are taken:
The only ones left are really not worth looking at.
Columbia is the only woman on earth who has not made
The definitive passive gesture, completely irreparable.

Al is ready to go to any lengths to keep her from being tricked.
For a virgin of her beauty, there are old, rich men who are
Ready to dish out hundreds of thousands of dollars.
Some big numbers make you shiver.

Hell's kingdom is tempting the ex-gangster.
To vanquish Satan, you need bombs,
And bombs are expensive.
Now, intact beauties of Columbia's caliber

Easily bring in a million a day
When they have the good sense to stay free-lance.
Electric Razor, take your toys and go home!
A duel with God is lost in advance.

XXXXXXXIII

In Electric Razor's room,
There is no air, but rather water.
It's like that not only in Electric Razor's room.
It's like that in all the rooms of Manna-Water.

That's why Electric Razor's rays
Are not in an aquarium, but in a cage.

In addition to the rays, those electric rays,
She has robins. The robins are not in a cage.

They are, of course, in an aquarium full of air.
Electric Razor has not eaten all day,
In order to love Columbia the haughty with greater appetite.
For she is sure that she will come give herself.

She waits and finds it a formidable wait.
In order to hold out against her, you've got to get up early,
For she can, because she has sold her soul to the devil,
Take on any shape and any color.

She can even make herself invisible.
Midnight is not far. She is confident.
She breaks a cross, spits on a Bible.
The force of her desire makes her vibrate

Like the string of a guzla, a Yugoslav guitar.
She has waited all her life without anything to wait for.
She has lived until now without having any desires.
And here she is, Hero waiting for Leander!

XXXXXXXIV

Columbia will go to the rendezvous with her revolver.
She will try to convert the she-devil.
It's midnight. She gets up. What a mess!
Columbia is in such distress!

She couldn't sleep either last night or the night before.
She opens the door. She sees no one.
Suddenly a laugh bursts out, as if spouting forth from hell.
She is frozen in place. She quivers and shivers.

"Electric Razor! Electric Razor! It's me!

Where are you? You're hiding, aren't you?"
"Do you want to or not? Make up your mind this second."
"Just a moment! Don't be in such a hurry!"

Electric Razor's teeth are as sharp
As the teeth of a saw. It's true.
With two strokes of her opposing jaws,
She has gobbled up Columbia's hands, up to the wrists.

In two seconds, she has eaten her cheeks,
Her eyes, her arms and even her legs.
Columbia fights back as would a madman.
The unattainable teeth continue to bite. The iambics

Of Paul Blablabla were less miserable.
Not to worry. She was able to activate her revolver before
Not having a single finger left on her hands to do it.
The invisible one was hit and sprays forth invisible blood
        everywhere.

XXXXXXXV

Before getting into the ambulance
That wants to take her to the hospital,
She is determined to express her gratitude
To the judge, to her ever so cordial host.

She crawls up into the little office.
With her back, she politely closes the door.
On her four stumps she bows.
"Before the attendants take me away,

I am anxious to tell you that I appreciate the
Hospitality you have shown me.
I cannot find the words, except thank you.
I would embrace you were I not so clumsy.

When I am old, I shall have a home of my own.
I do hope so. One never knows.
I invite you there. You shall be received like a king.
Does what I'm telling you displease you?

I shall sacrifice my fattest hen.
I shall uncork my oldest bottle.
In order to let you pass, I shall hold back the crowds.
Your eyes and ears will be blown away."

No word fell from the throat of the gray-matter-less one.
With both hands the judge fumbles, gropes and rips open her
    bodice,
Shakes her upper body like a flea trunk.
He is crazy with anger, hatred, fury and rage.

XXXXXXXVI

At the hospital, with electronic tools,
They do more than repair what she has that's broken.
They replace her lungs with pneumatic pumps
And screw them onto someone by the name of Scues-me,

An oil king whose breathing is stuffed up
By cigar and cigarette smoke,
Whose son doesn't stop burping
And whose daughter is named Arthurette.

They take her kidneys, which are intact,
And they give them to a breeder of automobiles.
One must be polite. One must use tact.
Especially when one is poor and an imbecile.

Her ovaries have not undergone a single bite.
They take them and solder them onto a movie freak.
He who gives to the rich lends to God. That's for sure.

They put her skin on a woman judge who has eczema.

The rich are not in favor of planting cabbage, you know.
Let's share: you plant them, we'll eat them.
It's no wonder the poor are calloused and pallid!
A few communist verses will please the angels

Of communism. At the hospital, they look at her blood.
It is beautiful, it is strong, it is healthy, it is red.
One must give one's blood to a better cause than oneself in
    one's time.
They inject it into a vampire worse than a tic called the Red
    Cross.

XXXXXXXVII

They fitted her with khaki eyes and lemon-yellow legs.
They set her up with the worst they had.
Don't throw the first stone at them, come on now!
When one hasn't worked hard in order to earn a pittance,

It is only fair that one be poorly treated at the hospital.
Columbia is glad, happy even, to be ugly-looking.
She no longer will give anyone the desire to do harm.
If the doctors had known, they would have tried even harder.

They would have chosen the most beautiful arms in the world,
Not the hairy, outrageously tattooed arms of a man.
Her hair is jet-black. Before, she was blond.
She had the voice of a mermaid. Now all she does is stutter.

Columbia does not find herself to be sufficiently ugly.
Hoist by your own petard, eh?
No one will ever again want to push her onto her hide-a-bed.
But Columbia is not always so lucky.

The notary has heard about her gratitude.
He does not hesitate. He's waiting for her at the hospital door.
"Come and have your convalescence at my house!"
Living in the water, sharks are clean. Long live the dirty ones!

They've stuck her with teeth so big
That she cannot open her mouth.
They deserve to be hanged!
Al has seen it all. A celestial beautician does some touching up.

XXXXXXXVIII

Little by little, she becomes herself again.
Horrible as she was, she no longer interested the dirty old men
Who pass their time, from Easter to Lent,
Waiting by the small end of a telescope

For her to lower her panties in order to pee.
To look through one of those small ends, you've got to have
        money
(Perhaps you won't want to believe what I say):
A million dollars a year.

Of course, it all goes to Al!
Pleasing the panty-peepers is expensive.
What is this world coming to? How ugly everything is!
I hear Marseilleans shouting: "Pshaw!"

All the maniacs are old geezers.
Those who run the world are all old:
No surprise that we're so near death.
Why, you say, is the world lame?

Because the age of those who run it is such that they limp!
Don't take me seriously.
I'm doing comic, not epic.

Laugh! Laugh! What? I'm doing my best!

Besides, the Union of Those in Stitches
Has voted a law requiring that spectators,
Like it or not, demonstrate pleasure
Even if it's boring. Do what the U.T.S. says. Hop to it!

XXXXXXXIX

The notary's boys and girls invite her
To join in a supposedly honest automobile rally.
Columbia says yes. Time flies. She's got to find
A friend fast. She's willing to risk her head.

The cellar is a shell made entirely of reinforced concrete.
And it's as big as the principality of Monaco.
That's where the event will take place. In order to be liked,
She is ready to eat nails and hammers.

They lend her an almost demolished six-cylinder.
They stick her with an automatic whose carburetor is all dirty.
The Chevrolet they supplied to her has cracked axles.
At the first rotation of the wheels, boom! the motor stalls.

They have fun; they treat her like a mental retard.
"What? You can't even drive?
So where were you born?
In Burundi? In Basutoland? Or worse?"

How to show them that she can do better?
Crying like a madwoman, humiliated and offended,
She manages to get the heap of iron going again.
Why in the world does everyone want to hurt her?

They give each other the word. They jump on the Chevrolet.
Three assaults, and all that's left is smoke and fire.

They laugh. They're licking their chops. Each one grabs a
    broom.
"Get out of that wreck so we can knock you around!"

XXXXXXXX

"You're looking for a friend?" asks Gaston, the notary's eldest.
"Well, here's one! Well, my friend, here I am!"
Under an almost sobbing willow, she was in the middle of reading
Voltaire. "Thanks!" she said. "What great joy you bring me!"

Columbia knows that they're still out to get her.
But she pretends there's nothing wrong.
Imagine if, through incredulity, she might deserve to be
    reproached
By that which governs the sealing of perfect ties.

"Teach me to be a friend!" continues good ol' Gaston.
"I know how to make love, but I don't know how to make friends.
Do we undress? Do you keep your slip on?
Do we perform humpbacked or on foot?"

In order to appear more sincere, he has taken crocodile
Tears and attached them to his eyelids.
"We begin," answers Columbia, "by surrendering our weapons;
We take down our tents; we stop being hard and proud.

Our masks are what we take off. Our hearts are what we unclothe.
We strip them bare so that each takes on the melody
Of the other's song: we'll be merrier than a terrier.
I'm ready to teach you what you have to do."

The conversation is recorded on tape.
Sipping cognac at supper, they play it.
They all scoff more than Hercules would.
Some of them end up with sore diaphragms.

XXXXXXXXI

The darkness is thicker than in a well.
In the bed that they've filled with lice and fleas,
Columbia scratches and scratches. A voice appeals to her.
"Stop going after the insects. You're killing more of them than
    the Russians

Killed Germans for the taking of Berlin!"
The voice is soft and deep. It comes from the heart of the night.
"Those parasitic apterous hemipteres come out of my hands.
Your attitude is intended to make me think that they're
    bothering you?"

"No, Lord! Oh, no! I didn't know!"
Suddenly, insane shouts ring out, as though emitted from hell.
It's the notary's boys and girls who are the authors of the
    pandemonium.
They're running out of ideas for bugging Columbia!

On the ceiling, suddenly, something opens like a trapdoor.
And out of it, amply, flows a thick, black molasses.
It has so much weight, it's so heavy, that it hits her
The way a billy goat knocks down a door. "Mercy! Mercy!"

She cries and it's as if she were losing her mind with each cry.
Having run out of molasses, they drop the down feathers,
Tons of sparrow and chaffinch feathers.
Columbia makes the sign of the cross and recites a Hail Mary.

XXXXXXXXII

She is called to justice. She is accused
Of having only verbally thanked
Her last host, the crafty notary.
All around her, the prosecutors and the lawyers, pleased,
Turn like flies around a honey pot.

The judge's gavel announces that the court is in session.
Paul Blablabla is happy to testify against her.
"To thank me, she threw a suitcase at my head!"

"Was the suitcase small, medium or large?"
"It was a weapon with a circumference of three feet.
It was full of vices, of balls and chains, and of dead
Bitches. Look: I am covered with putrid bruises."

"What does the accused have to say in her defense?"
"He had threatened me with a big revolver!"
"Why did he want to kill you? France,
In 1939, was right to threaten its adversaries.

Might you have humiliated, could you have offended
The excellent founder of Manna-Earth?"
"She didn't want to let me kiss her!"
The court rises up, red with anger.

"What?" cries the judge. "You would have refused him that
          small pleasure?
Since when does one take the liberty of not helping one's
          neighbor?
Down on your knees, quickly, and may your repentance be true!
You are sentenced to washing floors at Drizzle's house!"

XXXXXXXXIII

Drizzle is none other than Onemost Hinfamous, the mayor.
You have seen him watching a megalomaniac six feet tall
Pass under a bridge twelve feet high made of iron.
At this moment, he is having his young spouse copy ninety-four
          times

These few lines produced by his pen:
"From the bottom of my heart I regret having called my hubby

Disgusting. In the future, even when I have a cold,
I shall flatter him as he wishes and will caress him as best I can."

He gives a brush and some soap to Columbia. "Scrub!
Don't worry about wearing out the tiles; they're made of asphalt!
Get it clean! If you can't take the scum off
With this brush, take it off with your tongue. The Maltese Cross

Was just awarded to me. It's a great honor!
Congratulate me! Show how impressed you are!"
"I am quite happy for you!" she says in all candor.
"You are indifferent! Mother Nature gave you

No passion, no specifically sentimental energy.
Lord, what a century. What a generation! Degenerates!
Bunch of knuckleheads! Damn it all! I don't care for any of it!"
Onemost puts his head in his hands and starts to cry.

Columbia scrubs the floors, scrubs, wears out her hands.
She would like to console the Onemost Hinfamous, the
       ex-Aristide.
But he scares her. She has the impression that he is unhealthy,
That he has, in place of a soul, a large basin full of fecal matter.

XXXXXXXXIV

"Love, what's it good for?
It's good for making songs!
Songs, what're they good for?
They're good for making millions!

Love, what's it good for?
It's good for making children!
Children, what're they good for?
They're good for making money,

They're good for buying records, cha cha cha!
Oh, record factories where the poopy babies will work
When they are adults, old fogies, pooped out!"
Little Ferdinand Caron has written quite a song!

The mayor's adopted son is ten years old.
It's a song from the Top 40.
It's sung by all the children.
It's a hit for Billy Langlade.

It's a big moneymaker.
It's a good milk-cow.
They've translated it into German.
Some Japanese businessmen

Are very interested in it; you can't beat that.
The disc-jockeys are pushing the rubbish hard.
Disc-jockey is in the American tongue, if you please.
This song is a masterpiss that's going to rake in big bucks.[23]

XXXXXXXXV

"Hello!" says Columbia nicely to the little Ferdinand.
"Another one who's scared stiff!" he responds with contempt.
Columbia doesn't know what to do. Even the children!
She can't take it anymore! What a culture she lives in!

"Shut your trap and scrub the floors!" adds Ferdinand.
"I'll work my tail off. I shall acquit myself completely
Of my debt to society." "You don't have any sense of greatness!
You disgust me! Scrubbing the floors...! Sheesh!
Only murder could rid humanity of cankers like you!
When I grow up, to do us all a favor,
I shall kill them, the spineless imbeciles like the one I see here!
When the Martians come, what in the world, Sweet Jesus,

What will men be like, what will we be like
If dumb blondes like you continue to multiply?
What would a lion be like if most lions, my dear,
Were eaten by mites? All you know how to do is obey and bend
    over!

How disgusting! Pure filth!"
Ferdinand has lent a modern novel to Columbia.
She could not read it. She never learned the alphabet.
She's one of those rare birds who doesn't know Jules Verne.

She only has a month to go of shaking out the doormat,
After which society (all human beings in their entirety)
Will permit her to come back to its tit.
Priests, electricians, all will say: "It's over. Take my hand!"

XXXXXXXXVI

What has she done to make everyone refuse her?
That question pounds in her head just as the philosopher
Marcuse's hammer hits the nail on the head.
They all laugh when she opens her heart, every single time,

As though clowns were coming out of it, real Ringling Brothers.
She turns over and over in her bed of stone.
It is as if she were obsessed. She can't seem to sleep.
Just what is so funny in her manner?

She goes into Ferdinand's room. She wakes him up.
"Ferdinand! Ferdinand! Why do you refuse my friendship?"
Without warning, he pops her ears
Four ringing times. He's as angry as a person of private means.

"Friendship? Aren't you ashamed? So you don't know
That it's with senseless words like those that humanity
Has become what it is? The end is near!

Don't you know that speaking of that inanity

Is worse than selling opium, that it's sowing the seeds of heresy?
Friendship! It's one of the pernicious inventions
Of the deadheads of Ancient Greece! Friends don't exist, any more
Than did Bacchus and Zeus!

If I told you: 'There is gold under my mattress,'
And if you didn't find any, what would you think of me?
You'd say: 'He wanted to take me for a ride,' right?
Ah, I can hardly wait for you to leave our house!"

XXXXXXXXVII

With a totally pontifical gesture,
Hinfamous plunges the soup spoon
Into the soup tureen made of gold.
He sees something that completely

Takes his breath away and disrupts his train of thought.
In the tureen, hopping and jumping around,
Are old wrinkled frogs
So thin that one can see their ribs.

And he had been ready to enjoy himself!
He is surprised in a spectacular way.
He has swallowed up his mustache.
Ferdinand is chuckling deep in his throat, behind his molars.

"It's the floor-washer!" says he.
"I swear it; I saw her do it!"
"Go get me that imbecile
So that I can quickly kick

Her butt as much as she deserves!
To think that we house, nourish and bleach that jerk!

Good Lord, pity has its limits!"
"Come on, Columbia! Come see Papa!"

And the poor girl follows the child.
"He has a beautiful surprise for you.
Is it a doll? Is it an elephant?"
She protests. She only did her duty. She is quite alarmed.

XXXXXXXXVIII

The mayor's young wife and Columbia chat about everything
In the big house whose tiles shine.
"Don't get married! Better to have a yoke around your neck
Than a ring on your finger, no matter what the Church thinks."

There is no animosity in her voice.
Columbia can't believe her ears.
She tells her about her visit to the Trojan ruins.
She runs through her trips to Paris.

Has she finally met a kindred spirit?
"Keep talking. You are so sweet with me.
What were you saying about that masseur?"
She opens wide the doors, takes off the roof.

The mayoresse is nothing but a talker.
She doesn't even see the little orphan.
Knowing that two ears are listening is enough.
There's no more heart in her than in a mine.

She adores seeing that people are listening to her be very unhappy.
She adores hearing herself speak sadly.
She sees herself in a film. She's a driveling old fool.
"I could have married a count. I would be a countess."

The others come back; she becomes mean again.

With a grin, she offers her a cigarette.
Columbia says thanks. She is quite pleased. The tobacco blows up.
Everybody laughs. The explosion has broken everything in her
    head.

XXXXXXXXIX

There's nothing left unbroken
In the skull of the unfortunate Columbia.
She lies on the clean linoleum, her eyes rolled back in her head.
The cigarette exploded like an atomic bomb.

They don't know what to do to get rid of her.
They put her in an old rotten carriage.
They throw her into a hideous ditch.
Little by little her body becomes covered with moss.

The dogs sniff her. The cats come to sniff her.
The insects that are cadaver-eaters have a taste.
She is still alive. It makes them vomit.
Got to talk about that with Mamouth the biologist.

The agents from the animal pound
Don't get involved. Mind your own business!
They only deal with cats and dogs. When it comes to
    medium-size crocodiles
And human beings, they couldn't care less.

As for society as a whole, it is made
To distribute unemployment insurance checks,
Not to take care of girls thrown into the muck.
For her, even the Wise Men wouldn't have gone out of their way.

Her cheeks have sunk into her jaws.
She has twenty different head wounds.
The street lights are putting on their evening gowns:

It is exactly seven minutes till seven.

XXXXXXXXX

The barber is an inveterate bachelor.
He sees her. He plugs up his nose parce que the smell.[24]
He puts her on his back. He brings her to his house.
To see whether she is still alive, he puts his hand on her heart.

He washes her properly. He puts pajamas on her.
He puts her into a bed stripped of bedbugs.
The barber is full of eczema pimples.
At the age of three, he fell from a cliff,

Which made him a hunchback and quite a pessimist.
He piles blankets onto Columbia.
She has to be kept warm. Evarist,[25]
His dog, will watch over her when Macamasse,

Goddess of lassitude, will have triumphed over him.
It is his head that the hen called for.
She had seen him shaving in the middle of the night,
A criminal offense in the eyes of the Barber's Union.

There is a lake, a lake of air, of course,
On the other side of Judge Hooker's hills.
Tomorrow, he will go to cast into it the twisted body
Of what is left of this young lady.

There is someone other than himself in his house.
The barber can't believe his old blue eyes.
A human nose other than his smells his house.
Will she sense that he is in love with her?

XXXXXXXXXI

Columbia regains consciousness. Where am I?
Pipe tobacco smoke is swirling around.
She sees the terrible barber. She freezes.
He is as ugly as a cat hanged by its intestines.

Silence. He asks her if she is hungry.
Columbia, despite her horror, smiles.
She makes eyes at him, despite her disdain.
If she only knew that he wants to become her husband!

She is so weak that she cannot raise her arms.
Before the door of her mouth a spoon appears
Full of fruits, vegetables and a fatted calf.
"Open your mouth and swallow. It's good! I found you the day
    before yesterday.

I'm the barber. Do you recognize me?
You're Christopher Columbus, aren't you?"
He awaits her response. He has ceased speaking.
"Yes... Well... Something like that."
He is as good and solicitous as a young abbot.
He lifts the spoon. She opens her mouth.
He talks to her as he would to a little baby.
"Lend me your nose so I can wipe it.

With me, you don't need to be afraid.
No one here will harm you."
She feels quite strange. She's scared.
She does not believe in the pity of Anastasius Valley.

XXXXXXXXXII

He is so nice to her
That she doesn't distrust him much anymore.
He has her get up on his merciless saddle.

He brings her to Mass, sleeps on the sofa.

People call him an old sex maniac. He shrugs.
At church, Columbia sees her rainbow ring
On one of the notary's fingers and finds it funny.
When one feels well, a dirty trick is just a joke.

She tells her story to the barber.
He listens to her carefully, then says to her, smiling:
"I can remember even worse.
Be powerful and tough like an elephant:

Strong enough to be able to smash through the greatest obstacles
And hard-headed enough to avoid getting hurt while smashing.
The difficult part is to pass through the show's scenery
Before they take you and keep you like cement."

Talk, Anastasius, but without saying that you love her.
Columbia listens to him fervently. He's such an easy-going man!
If he spoke without wisdom, she would appreciate him anyway.
She's in no hurry to find herself on the road again.

"When you feel cured, you tell me.
I'll give you a little bread and a little money.
You'll say good-bye to me and you'll leave."
How ardently would he have children with her!

XXXXXXXXXIII

He asks her whether she is cured.
She answers that her head aches.
She's lying. She wants to stay with him.
She wants the party to last.

She spends her time washing the floors,
The ceilings, the walls and the dog.

She wants him to think she's devoted.
She wants him to tell her that she cleans well.

The copper doorknobs, she scrubs 'em.
She sands down the back of the drawers.
She works like an idiot.
She hums from morning to night.

"You're as busy as a bee
And you claim that you're suffering,
That you're still too fragile
To climb up the slightest slope."

When Anastasius addresses her so sharply
Columbia trembles like a leaf.
He's going to chase her away. He's going to kick her out the door.
She lowers her head, tears in her eyes.

But she has understood that he senses that she does not love him
    enough
To become what she has guessed that he wants her to be: his wife.
How she suffers from the awareness that this never stops
    hurting him!
He has told her: "As for children, I'd like to have twelve of them."

XXXXXXXXXIV

"In your place, white bird, I would be eager
To spread my wings."
He caresses her knee, taps it.
If she liked that, he'd be a happy man.

"I am a crow and I am paralyzed."
Downtown, gossip is spreading like wildfire.
Haircuts are really in these days!
People come in the morning. At noon, they're back.

They want to see the sex maniac at work.
They want to catch him in the act.
They want to see the old bastard
Do the dastardly deed with the pretty maiden.

They see Columbia sweeping up the hair.
That's all they can find to nibble on.
People don't always get to see what they want to.
Sometimes, you don't get what you paid for.

Columbia picks up lots of shorn hair.
She carefully sharpens the razors.
Columbia helps the balding man
Put on his black tailcoat.

That guy is wearing a mink pelt.
Columbia is courteous to them all.
For her, the customer is always right.
In the cash register, there's plenty of change.

XXXXXXXXXV

"You're leaving tomorrow morning. We talk; we shoot the breeze,
And I don't have any more sentimental patience.
He can hardly stand it anymore, your old Anastasius.
Have you heard of the tantalizing torture of Tantalus?"

The more he sees her, the more his yearning grows.
She is so young; she'd be so good to take.
Why are some provided with ugliness?
Why is it not enough to show great tenderness?

"Go on, starting from where I found you.
Go! Leave! Quickly! Or else I'm going to believe
That you have no more heart than a private chauffeur.
Out you go! As for me, I'm going to hit the bottle.

Who are you? Stop bawling.
Leave! Or else I shall believe that you are a parasite,
That your ambition is to eat without working.
Clear out! You've got to earn them,

Your bread, your salt, your butter, your hearth and your bed."
Tears streaming down her face, Columbia throws herself into
    his arms.
"How can you be so cruel, my friend?
The love I have none of, perhaps it will be born."

The sheriff comes in. He sees it all.
He snaps pictures. He gets out his handcuffs.
He's more than a little proud of his coup.
"Come along, Anastasius. The crazy kid's kisses are a thing of
    the past!"

XXXXXXXXXVI

He is accused of having fooled around.
As for proof, everybody's hands are full of it.
Stones have been thrown through all the windows.
They hanged him at five-thirty this morning.

Doubled over under the weight of the grief,
She takes up once again the wheel of fortune.
She is once again alone on the way.
A wasp stings her right in the eye.

"My God! Support me! Help me!
Capone, I don't know what to do anymore!"
How ugly this route seems to her.
What a high price must be paid for joy.

At the violet lintel of the door of Manna,
The old barber's body sways.

Vultures circle all around.
Everything smells rotten to her.

She wants to talk to someone.
That's quite a normal impulse.
Whether we're drunk or fasting,
When we're grieving, that's what we all want to do.

It's too much to bear.
She drops to the ground under the lintel
Of the door of Manna, drops
To the ground under the lintel of the door of Manna-Water.

XXXXXXXXXVII

She knocks on the door of the rectory,
A fifty-one-story building.
"Hello, little wretch. How may we help you?"
She wants to see the priest. "Is it for a wedding?"

No. It's to help her get out of her despair.
"If that's all it is, the priest is busy.
Come back later. Come back one of these evenings."
Columbia says that she'll be back at suppertime.

She knocks again at the palace door.
The maid cries out: "Ah! It's you again!"
His Eminence is not yet ready to receive her.
He has lots to do. He's up to his neck in work.

Columbia says that she will try around nine o'clock.
She presents herself once again at the door to the building.
"I need help. I have a sword in my heart."
"As in the song by Crosby Bing?"

Columbia lies down on the church square; she falls asleep.

The sun comes up again. The servant wakes her up.
"You're like a bitch, 'cause you sleep outdoors."
She picks her up, a bit by the hair, a bit by the ears.

She roughs her up by twisting her arm.
She tells her to leave her boss alone.
"The Reverend is busy! Go away! Go on!
Nymphets like you give him heartburn."

XXXXXXXXXVIII

For six months, the reverend priest has been married.
He has married a little woman with a big rear end.
For six months, the reverend priest has been overwhelmed.
Only by forcing himself does he have time to say his Masses.

Between his Masses, he is constantly creating children.
He hasn't had time to see each of their faces.
All in all, he has thrown into the world three thousand two
        hundred of them.
Between two children, to perk himself up, he eats molasses.

He doesn't see anyone anymore. Like a Protestant, he leaves
The sinners to confess directly to our dear God.
He is swamped with work. The regular customers,
The little old ladies, he sends elsewhere for confession, and not
        to heaven, either.

His sermons are not long. "Love one another!
Off to bed! Add and multiply!"
After the Mass, he runs out like a real crazy man.
He's got to find her again, his spouse, his spermtray.[26]

As for the wretches, he hasn't the time to receive them anymore.
When they insist, he has someone give them a bottle.
There lies within some gray milk: vile, impossible to drink.

At two o'clock in the morning, he wakes up his wife!

He has promised himself not to let his spouse go without work.
In the evening, to keep her from falling asleep too soon,
He gives her No-doze anti-soporifics.
You can hear the wailing all the way to Montevideo, capital of
    Uruguay.

XXXXXXXXXIX

She leaves Manna, never to return.
After all this time seeing it through the water, she has forgotten
The sun's brilliance. She almost faints.
What brightness! She ties her shoes resolutely.

She crosses the river, sets foot on Wother.
You can't start from scratch without confessing, taking
    communion
And addressing a few "Our Fathers" to the Virgin Mary.
Joanna has come back to life. With a big basket under her arm,

She is collecting whales on the beach.
Joanna is the mother of Paul Blablabla and of his brother.
Columbia asks Joanna whether the latter, a wise cleric,
Is still the priest of Wother.[27] She is sullen and proud.

"What's wrong with my little Paul that you don't like him?
Who do you think you are? The Princess of Wales?
He doesn't have nice enough legs, nice enough arms?
All in rags and thinks she's France Gall!"

Joanna tosses crustaceans at Columbia, hits her
Hard on the nose with her wicker container.
What a scandal! The telephone rings at the home of Miss Johnson.
"And don't go bothering my other son during his breakfast!"

The Wother rectory is all cracked, all decrepit.
It looks like Jesus on the cross, in the midst of his suffering.
She runs to it like a bird to its nest.
Some structures inspire confidence!

XXXXXXXXXX

The Wother priest's goodness mends her broken heart.
She is comforted by his gracious ways.
She tells him her tale of woe.
Then she says to him: "Tell me: what must I do?"

He taps his alert thighs twice.
He clicks his long, green, fat tongue.
All the while he chews on mint Dentyne
Because he's afraid that his breath smells bad.

He doesn't seem to know quite what to say.
Suddenly, like a child, he applauds.
He claps his hands: he could have done worse.
Al inspired him. God told him what to say.

"My child, you have looked for friendship
In the heart of human beings.
In order to be loved by them, you've tried everything;
You've moved heaven and earth.

And you've failed. And everything has been set against you.
Must your soul bleed until death?
No! Drop them. They're not the only ones on earth.
Have you ever spent time with beings from another kingdom?

There are animals, by the hundred thousands.
There are cats, dogs, wolves, flies.
Think of the lions, the boas, the tortoises, the boars.
Try them. You'll see. They're not so ferocious."

XXXXXXXXXXI

Between Ruffville and the Bodes-Ill Mountains,
Columbia meets a big dog with long white hair,
An animal that has hair all over its face.
She'll see whether animals are so wonderful.

Like her, his head is down and he's no prize winner.
"Come, Johann Sebastian Bark! Come, Johann Sebastian Cur!
We'll sleep under the stars on the same straw.
I'll be nice. I'll never stop telling you that you're handsome."

She runs after the big dog. He escapes, galloping.
The faster she pursues him, the faster he flees.
Suddenly, she trips on a big, beautiful, mauve bone.
"Look what I've found." A bone, that excites them,

Especially when it's of that color.
Tail between his legs, head down,
Quite troubled by the sight of the succulent meal,
The digitigrade walks toward the one who wanders ceaselessly.

As soon as he gets to within arm's reach,
She grabs him, caresses him, flatters him, massages him.
"We'll stay together. We won't leave one another.
Are you a mongrel or a thoroughbred?"

She places the pink bone at his feet. He takes it with his teeth.
He turns his back on her. No! She begs him to follow her.
"Is that what you call gratitude?"
It is difficult to win the love of a dog as white as frost.

102

She wakes up in a barn. He is gone.
She is angry, but she is not surprised.
He seemed to follow her walking backwards. Fuckin' A!

She goes out. Erect and disappointed in the gray light

Of a fine rain, she reflects; she wonders.
Across the forest, there is only one path.
He must have taken it. She brushes off her old gown
To remove the bits of straw. He has repudiated her!

Cursing in Huron, she starts to look for him.
She walks until noon, continues until the evening.
To see better, she perches on top of a pine tree.
Worn out, she takes advantage of it to sit down.

She meets a man with a gun. He's a hunter.
"Have you seen my big dog along the way?"
He looks at her and starts to laugh like a joker.
"I murdered one of them a little while ago.

You'll find him about a fifteen-minute walk from here.
I saw him. I aimed. Zap! A single bullet.
You'll pick him out very easily." "Good-bye and thank you."
She leaves him, sensing that he wants to harm her.

She begins to run. Dead or not, she'll cure him.
The hunter fires. He misses her. Ka-pow!
He misses her again. He's a true villain.
Our globe-trotter slips away like a fawn.

103

She finds the animal. He's black with blood.
She carries him in her arms. She sniffles, cries.
A malfunctioning plane skims past her as it crashes.
In life, you see a little bit of everything.

In a stable, she makes a big fire.
She spreads him out at the foot of the flames, wraps him up.

She looks for the hole made by the weapon of the raving mad
    hunter.
"Poor Johann Sebastian Bark, I'll give you back your breath."

With a forceps, she pulls out the bullet.
With salt water, she cleans the wound.
With little strips of percale,
She washes his coat and gives it back its sheen.

"What can I do to bring you back to life, Johann Sebastian Cur?"
She thinks of the bundle of moonbeams
Attached to the bottom of each body of water.
She looks under the frozen rain, finds a brown rivulet

Obscured by a thick rhododendron bush.
Inside the building the fire has gone out. She starts it again.
She puts one of the magic beams into the dead dog's snout.
"It's good! Eat it up!" She coughs. She has caught a cold.

The beam melts on his tongue and mixes with the blood.
Victory! The dog has wagged his tail!
She sings. There are no songs cheerful enough,
No refrains joyous enough.

104

How happy Columbia is! She has shed her bitterness!
How handsome he is! How affectionate! How crafty!
When he pants with his mouth open, you'd think he's laughing.
Columbia is so free and easy with Johann Sebastian Bark!

Sometimes, he follows in her footsteps, angling for a pat.
Other times, he lags behind, playing with the telephone poles,
Then catches up to her, breaking all speed records.
He glimpses some shimmering fresh water at the bottom of a
    small hill:

He goes rushing off to drink and comes back galloping at top
    speed.
He is never tired. He has a joyous way of walking.
He walks as though he were dancing. He lifts his paws high.
He never stops pricking up his long, frizzy ears.

He moves them all the time, like the wings of a bird.
What is that noise, he always seems to say.
He's a certified yapper. He barks at everything, especially cars,
Sometimes clouds, wind, smoke from a boat.

When a motor vehicle passes by,
He's hot on its tail at top speed.
He scolds, shouts. He defies them. He threatens them.
My word, it's as though he were a pussycat.

Those machines are little chicks to him.
He cannot explain them to himself otherwise.
He thinks that they are afraid, that they go fast because they're
    fleeing.
He looks at Columbia as if to say: "It's running away, the
    scaredy-cat!"

105

She sleeps on drowsy flowers, on a midnight field.
Johann Sebastian licks her once on the mouth.
"Come see!" It's with gestures that he says what he has to tell her.
She's off. He brings her to the ditch where he gave birth.

Surprise! He has delivered! And how!
He's had four puppies! They're shivering all over!
Columbia welcomes them as one would a president.
They look like drowned cats! How annoying!

"Oh! Johann Sebastian Cur! Oh! Johann Sebastian Bark!

You old smarty-pants! You little devil! Lie down on them for a
　　　while!
They're dying of cold, don't you see? Aren't they hungry?
Lie down! There! Make them comfortable! What's the use of
　　　being hairy

Like you if it's not to keep newborns warm?"
Columbia takes off her dress and covers the dog and the little ones.
How cute they are! Her head is buzzing at the thought of it.
There's an indigo one, a fuchsia one, a vermilion one and a gray
　　　one.

Look how she's no longer alone! How she fits in with them!
Now there are six of her, more numerous than the trees in a forest
When the heart of a summer has set fire to it.
There are so many of her that a legion would retreat!

106

On the highway, between Los Angeles and San Antonio,
Everything is for the best in the best of all worlds.
But only three of the four little Curs are left.
The vermilion one got run over by an otherworldly machine:

A cement mixer of a yellow hue verging on khaki
That didn't even seem to notice,
That didn't do anything, didn't even slow down.
It's really too cruel. Pass me your handkerchief.

Its brothers have changed: they are much more prudent.
When they feel like doing a little discovering,
Without hesitating, they head toward the fields.
In every cloud, there's a silver lining – it goes without saying.

Every morning Columbia brushes their teeth well.
When there's a dairy nearby, it's party time with milk.

She steals sugar cubes for them in restaurants.
"May I use the bathroom, please?"

She beats them good and hard when she's got to beat them.
There's no such thing as a puppy that you don't have to
        reprimand.
"Come here so I can brush you, so I can wash your paws."
She's as proud of them as Marie-Jeannette of Holland

Was proud of her son, the emperor Alexander II.
If you don't like my comparisons, return the book.
It will be a pleasure to refund you your three dollars and two cents.
Columbia is drunk with motherly love.

107

Quite often, there's nothing to eat or drink.
Then the little ones cry out after her, raising their heads.
They are so pitiful that she falls into despair.
Where are the cups full to the brim and the heaping plates?

She's got to do something. She thinks about it.
They have a right to three square meals a day, like everyone else.
It's not their fault that they're stuck with an ill-equipped mother.
She watches a hundred round-cheeked poodles go by.

"What are we going to do, Johann Sebastian Bark?
We won't let them perish, will we?
We are not criminals or assassins."
They want milk. There are plenty of cows.

But all of the cows belong to someone.
But God made the bovine creatures and the earth nourishes them.
Now, to whom does this globe belong if it is not to each and
        every one?
The first Jersey she sees, she's off with it. Too bad!

Those who have sixty cows have stolen sixty cows!
Without knowing it, she's reasoning like Fourier.[28]
It's not very pretty. Don't cast the first bone.
She's in dire straits. What would you do?

108

They take small steps across the Utah desert.
The climate is torrid. Speed is out of the question.
The spotted cow brings up the rear, clip-clop.
It's having a hard time. "Calm down, children!"
It bellows what it has to say to them.
A cow is simply enormous. Columbia is proud to have it.
To possess a more voluminous being than oneself is like getting
     bigger.
She rests her head on one of its black blotches

And it's as though she were putting it on the slope of a mountain.
Like all heavy things, it is tranquil and solid.
In her torn dress, like Tarzan in his loincloth,
Columbia moves ahead with a joy that is anything but sordid.

She knocks on doors to get a gallon of water.
A little of this liquid and a little grass from here and there are
     enough for it.
When it puffs like a steer, it's too hot,
And to drink an ounce it would do something stupid.

Meanness is the mistress of the gas pump attendant who refuses
     water
For a cow, for a living being with a head and heart.
"Mister Pump Attendant, my cow is hot, incredibly hot.
A cup, a full glass, and its satisfaction will be complete."

"No! Beat it or I'll call the police."
"Thank you. You could not have pleased me more."

Kneeling down on the asphalt, she prays. The call to evening
    prayer sounds.
Her friends are intrigued. They try to read her mind.

109

A truck exporting pork chops
Passes by at top speed, dropping a barrel.
Crazy as can be, the little ones run after the barrel that twists,
That rolls to the middle of the clean, flat asphalt.

"Come back here! Right now!" shouts Mother Columbia.
Seduced by the odor of the meat, the little ones hear nothing.
Suddenly, from the horizon, appears, zooming at the speed of a
    bomb,
A little automobile the brilliant color of red wine.

Columbia runs after the little ones who run after the chops.
The latter roll more quickly than the former who run more
    quickly than she.
If she had some money, she would get handcuffs
And her little ones would not be at the mercy of the sparks

Of the spark plugs of that triple-carburetor Austin.
Look at Johann Sebastian Cur, scratching himself tranquilly!
But the cow has seen it all, grasped the meaning and she has heart.
She waits a bit. The moment has not yet come.

The danger having become extreme, she leaps, rushes in.
She sits in the middle of the highway, between her friends and
    the killer car.
Legs apart, she rises up like a monolith
Between her companions and the furious machine.

Bang! The little automobile, like a gun shot,
Hits the cow, which like a wall, does not give way.

The little automobile, like a thrown ball, rebounds,
Then it breaks into tiny pieces, like a chocolate rabbit.

110

In the thick sand of the Utah desert,
Columbia settles in to sleep a good while.
The cow serves as a pillow. Big fat Queen Victoria
Is not better off on her throne than Columbia is on her
    halter-less friend.

Up high in the darkness rockets are shining.
Stones soar upward like human beings all around.
In American deserts, a pale, greenish sagebrush grows
Which shines in the night like iron works in the oven.

At the heart of the rock peaks, it's as if she were on the moon.
The sand gets colder. Underneath the cold, a little warmth is left.
Johann Sebastian is cleaning up. With his long brown tongue,
He washes All-Fuchsia, All-Grey and All-Indigo.

Since one can't see a thing, he washes them by heart.
It's Columbia's turn! Beforehand, he sniffs her.
She's pretending to be asleep. He's all gentleness.
He gives her licks as brutal as slaps.

He cleans her face. He files her fingernails.
It would make anyone else nervous.
He lies down on her stomach, his muzzle spread out under her
    breasts.
Is she bestial? That kind of confession is for later!

Tapping her under the nose with one last lick,
Johann Sebastian Cur makes Columbia sneeze.
The sound of the explosion startles the others.
She laughs. "It's only me; it's not an atomic bomb."

111

There are ten of her now. The cow has had twins.
She had them in the lower courtyard of a female farmer
Who did everything to make the labor go smoothly.
To go into Albuquerque, one must go down Mount Saltshaker.

To get out of it, one climbs Mount Peppershaker.
The bird breeder is a little cynical, but she's kind.
She attaches little bells that ring gaily
Around the necks of yesterday's barely born animals.

"My girl, you must have bats in your belfry!"
Says the Albuquerquese woman to the traveling orphan.
"You've lost some of your marbles, huh? Or else you're tipsy.
Do you really plan to drag around this fur club all your life?"

Columbia says yes. It's natural to bring along one's buddies.
"And ten, that's still not enough for you, I bet!
Just what will you look like at the head of this cowshed out on
     the highways?
Well, I'd be ashamed! This is no way to catch a husband!"

She is cynical, but generous like the earth.
She keeps them for a week. They eat what they want.
She's as big as a barrel and has a penchant for beer.
Although old, she's neither a bigot nor a prude.

It's time to say farewell. Everyone is sentimental.
"My girl, I like you; I want you to remember me."
Saying this, she hands her two large suitcases, two trunks.
"Open them!" Columbia almost dies of love and joy.
In one, there's a feline and in the other a goose.

112

The name of the cat is Unconstitutionally.
He's not an ordinary cat; he is unique in the world.
Tired of walking, he jumps, quickly, athletically,
On the back of one or another and, like a ship on the waves,

He lets himself be carried, as though that were all that needed to
    be done.
He knows how to talk to ants. Unconstitutionally
Is a word in a dead dialect, in a cemetery language,
Which signifies: great friend of the Hymenoptera. It's astonishing!

Pauline-Émilienne[29] walks like Hitler's soldiers.
There's nothing fascist about that; she's a goose.
She lays eggs without shells and without whites,
Eggs full of sweet juice, jam or nuts.

She is even whiter than Johann Sebastian Bark.
Her beak is more yellowy orange than the fruit itself.
Her eyes, black like jade, are as little as dots.
Truly, she's just the kind of bird one likes.

She always walks a mile ahead of them.
This bad habit makes Columbia tremble with fear.
"You'll get yourself stolen and eaten by some beggar.
So stay with us! Do you think you're a scout?"

Her webbed feet are equally yellowy orange.
She waddles as she walks, like a false ingenue.
Instead of talking, she trumpets. Does that bother you?
Birds like that aren't a dime a dozen.

113

Between St. Louis and Chicago,
Red knolls resembling Mount Pelée and Mount Kumamoto
Stand on the shoulder in the gray dust.
In these little volcanoes, some very lively insects are moving.

The ants go into their anthills as if going into a mill.
They enter ceaselessly in procession.
How hurried they seem! On metropolitan boulevards,
There is no more coming and going than around these elevations

Constructed of grains culled from deep underground.
They work (what a bad example they set!)
Endlessly, just as blood flows in your arteries.
The minuscule pebble gets put down without any fuss,

As one places a potato on a pile of spuds
Then, without downing any coffee, zig-zagging in order not to hit
The avalanche that's coming, making haste not waste,
They dive back into the hole as thin as a mending thread,

African[30] and more cramped than the hollow of a straw.
The dog yaps. The bird whistles. Like fish,
Ants make no sound. The peacock squawks.
Man is a glutton for pessimistic songs.

Then Unconstitutionally sits down,
His nose above a crater, and meows.
The ants raise their heads. They see him.
And they speak to one another in silence about eating, and war,
     and willows...

114

Inspired by horses, the cat tries his hand at transportation.
He's got his friends, the three ants, on his nose,
Which is pink like candy from Chandernagor,[31]
Like a bit of chewing gum from the south of the Pyrenees.

The nostrils of the cat are like craters.
The ants called Bic, Fic and Vic feel right at home there.
You still don't know the cow's name. It's Mooma.
Now you've got the picture! That was a close call!

The three sisters are less timid than at the start.
They don't go into Mooma's nostrils. Too hot!
But those of the others, they frequent them frequently.
One mustn't sneeze. If you do, it's adios amigo.

It's over. They won't look at you anymore. Not a word!
No more tickling! The most profound contempt!
You have insulted them. You've got to get up early
If you want them to forgive you, to forget it.

Three ants, they don't chow down.
They don't eat in a fearful and atrocious way.
You can nourish them ten years with the capital of one penny.
They're not like everybody else, always sitting down to eat.

Then Unconstitutionally catches a rat.
Quite proud, he bites it. The rodent's bones crack.
Columbia beats the hunter and takes the poor little thing in her
        arms.
She hugs it, puts it to sleep on her heart. "You are Shalac."

115

At San Angelo, a little mining and border town
In a State of the U.S.A. where coyotes abound,
They witness an extraordinary spectacle,
As uncommon as middle C, the note;

As unusual as a fish swimming.
Around the fountain a noisy crowd has gathered.
"Why are they going to hang him?" asks the calf named Bleater.
"A union scandal!" answers his sister called Badger.

"I don't understand any of it!" cries Bic.
"I'd lose my Latin over it if I had any."
"Look! It's horrible! I'll be gosh-darned!
They're putting the cord around his neck! What did he do?"

Bleater asks Badger to bellow to him clearly
What that tiny little bald human being has done.
The town councilors all seem to be quite happy.
The trap door of the scaffolding opens. Pauline-Émilienne vomits.

Fic goes to find the handsome Unconstitutionally.
"Do *you* understand any of this? I'm totally lost!"
"He's a farmer who organized a move."
"So what? That's bad? Just let me at 'em, I'll move 'em!"

"How ignorant! To have the right to move,
You must be part of the movers' union…"
He is hitched up among the oranges of an orange tree
For having carried his refrigerator himself.

116

The fifteen or sixteen animals think somberly
About the tragic scene that they have just witnessed.
They discuss it in short phrases, almost in silence.

To understand one another, they don't need to shout.

"Our lives are not in any danger.
The union police have no jurisdiction over us.
We have to think about our poor Columbia.
We mustn't forget that she is human, like those crazy ones."

"Bic is right," says All-Fuchsia. "If they grab her,
We'll end up using a spoon to pick up what's left.
The dog who had that bald man, he lost him.
If we don't want to lose Columbia that way…"

"There aren't enough of us," claims Mooma.
"If there were a thousand of us, let's say, she would be safe.
Our united teeth must be able to bite the earth.
There are not enough of us. I have spoken."

"Mooma speaks well," says Pauline-Émilienne.
"We should bring along all of our buddies with us.
Not the praisers! Not the wanderers!
The glowering ones! The earnest ones! The supertough ones!"

"There will be thousands of us!" they say to one another, dreamily.
We're ready for anything in order to save our leader.
We'll fight them down to the last drop of their blood.
We'll stuff their scaffoldings down their dry throats."

117

In Baltimore, terminus of Highway 33,
They decide to declare a vacation.
All the more so because the goose has laid three pre-geese,
A trio of eggs that she must cover with her belly.

Can she be expected to brood while walking?
All along the streets full of cars and trucks,

They seek a temporary yet welcoming residence.
To think that there are some who have a chalet in addition to a
    house!

They venture into the municipal dump.
Shalac, shouting: "Yippee!" jumps off his mistress's shoulder.
To a rat, nothing is more beautiful than dirty waste products.
When this rodent is in the midst of squalid rubbish, he is jubilant.

The town dump spreads over acres.
They find what they were looking for in order to put down roots:
A streetcar still full of the acrid smell
Of the fire that licked it, that cooked it.

It's a marvel! The door is spacious enough
To let the cow through. Way at the back,
A sort of padded, almost luxurious esplanade
Will permit them to sleep like Philippe Entremont.

Concert pianists have very soft beds.
They are enchanted and show their pleasure.
They sing. They dance. They jump. They laugh.
For them, this burned-out trolley is a streetcar named desire.

118

Most rats have set up shop in sewers.
In those of Baltimore, Shalac spent his childhood.
He emigrated by chance, a truck full of cabbage
Having taken off without warning.

He goes to see his pals. He gets a blow to the heart.
They have all changed. They have trouble recognizing him.
There are even some who stand up
As if to start a fight with a traitor.

"Remember!" he cries. "Open your eyes!
Truly, Capone has not spoiled me in the
siblings department! Anne! Lisa! Paul! Matthew!"
They excuse themselves. They're sorry. They make peace.

They give him a big piece of rotten cheese.
To Shalac, there's nothing better than that.
They drink dishwater until they're tipsy.
"Nothing goes to your head faster than that sink-juice!"

Finally, everyone being quite at ease,
He begins to speak about Columbia, his mistress.
"She is beautiful. She is fresh as the morning dew!
And she loves us. And she never stops praising us."

He tells them that she reconciles all the animals.
"If you come, she'll be as happy as a fool!
She was born in May, the month of Gemini!"
They're off like children behind their schoolmaster.

119

They go to the movies. The little ones go in through the
    basement windows.
Secrecy is more difficult for the big ones.
It is possible. They're proving it right now.
They don't have a penny. They don't have any money.

They lean forward so that the ushers won't catch them.
The ushers go back and forth armed with a big stick.
Fortunately, they are as near-sighted as they are mean,
And at the movies, it's not as light as it is on the sidewalk.

It's a story in color about cowboys and Indians.
The cow and his buddies applaud the feathered warriors.
The starlet is very made-up, very faithful and very well-behaved.

The Sioux who try to get her to… receive overwhelming blows.

"Go get yourself hugged somewhere else, headshrinker!
If you touch me, I'll sic my big dog on you!"
"Stop devouring her with your eyes, coward, thief, womanizer!"
"I can't always stare at the left bank of the Rhine!"

The star and the starlet, in the moonlight,
Tickle each other while exchanging lots of words.
Columbia is not impressed by the kisses on the dunes.
She only has eyes for the faces of their horses.

The horses make her think of big beautiful women,
Of tall baronesses, of haughty grand-duchesses.
She looks at the horses, her eyes full of flames.
For a single horse, she'd give up her whole youth.

120

On the sidewalk, Columbia finds some glasses.
With a measured gesture, she puts them on her nose.
The calves bellow. The dogs yap. The goose trumpets.
They make so much noise! Satan wouldn't even recognize the
    damned.

She says yes, fine. She'll always wear them.
She looks so wise with lenses on!
They surround her expression with velour.
She looks like Nana Mouskouri.[32] The crowd exaggerates.

Everyone licks her and congratulates her.
"Don't throw any more kisses! Enough! I'm up to my ears!"
They're beautiful and pretty but, in the long run, they irritate
Her false khaki eyes; they give her a migraine.

Courageously, she doesn't take off the glasses.

She never complains. She doesn't have the right to.
My God, my Al, how her head aches!
But, to make them giggle, nothing is

Too painful, too difficult, too hard.
When Shalac came up to her with all his buddies,
She exploded with joy. "This is no way to go!
Pretty soon we're all going to die of starvation!"
Then the goose came to offer her three little ones to her.
"If you don't stop that, I'll throw myself into the water!"
And the cat's belly is getting fatter by the day.
And Vic shows up with a fly in need of healing on his back.

121

When deliveries of merchandise arrive at the dump, they watch
    them.
The more there are in the group, the more grub is needed.
One time, they found a flask full of juice of the vine.
Unconstitutionally came up with a beautiful sweater:

Of course, it's Columbia who has inherited it.
A man comes up to the gate, all in tears.
It's the owner of a zoo who's five feet tall
And he's carrying his zoo like a bouquet of flowers.

"What is he doing here with that thing in his arms?"
Not believing her eyes, the goose goes to get the whole gang.
"He's going to throw out some animals, that fat little man!"
"You're dreaming or you've been drinking. We wonder which."

The goose didn't see double. Pauline-Émilienne told the truth.
Clutching his property, the little zoo owner
Is headed toward the main pit. Suppose Columbia were to speak
    to him.
"Go ahead. Don't spare him. Tell him he's nuts!"

Columbia catches up to him just at the edge of the abyss
Where he seems to want to drop his animals.
"What's gotten into you? Do you have verse in your rhymes?"
Everyone applauds. She didn't mince words with him!

The old cluck throws himself into their friend's arms.
"Madam, I cannot do otherwise: a union decree."
Her glasses on sideways, Columbia receives the zoo as a gift.
"If you want it, here it is. Don't do them any harm."

122

The zoo is like the owner: it's small.
In a way, it is as minuscule as a pill.
In others words, it's not heavily populated.
You don't need to be good in math

To carry out the census of its inhabitants.
There's a rhinoceros, a giraffe and a heron.
They receive them as if there were a hundred of them.
The name of the heron is quickly found: Nero.

"The giraffe really doesn't seem too swift!"
Thinks Columbia, who has become larger than a city.
"A sheep's head at the end of a telephone pole!
May I call you Imbecile?"

In vain, Columbia has been as well-intentioned as an abbess;
Standing under the giant, she feels no affection for him inside.
Then, like the arm of a mechanical crane, its neck comes down.
And she receives a rough lick under her nose.

The rhinoceros, Sweetie-Pie, is as ferocious as can be.
For fear of losing him, regretfully, they leave him in the cage.
He does not want to be friends. Nay! He charges at anything.

The ants slide along his white cheese horns.[33]

123

Bic, the ant, is in seventh heaven with Quadrimotor, the fly.
She says to her: "Land here and let's play world war!"
The fly lands and the ant lies down on her back.
The wings of the dipteran beat the way the propeller blades
Of a fighter plane turn in the heat of the action.
Over the trees, over the highest houses,
They pass by dragonflies and pow pow pow!...
The tale of their adventures can be found in a few almanacs.

Bic and Quadrimotor sleep together.
I think you're nice; you think I'm nice. It's perfect.
Besides, in physiognomy, they resemble one another,
As *scented menthol* resembles *sentimental*.

The march without a goal and without a destination has begun
      again.
They are on the way to Charleston, port of the Carolinas.
The cars that meet them make fun of them and laugh.
"Do you want brats? I've got a car full!"

It only makes Columbia sing: "Shepherd girl..."
The inflexible rhinoceros follows, a hundred rats on its back.
"If you don't want to follow, feel free, my dear."
In order not to be separated from the giraffe, he'll do whatever
      he has to.

Might as well follow these nitwits rather than stay
And renounce a camaraderie twenty years in the making.
He speaks to no one. He's kind of stubborn.
He minds his own business. He walks, head down, sluggish.

124

Theater disgusts me even more than trombones.
Bunch of screamers! Bunch of ear-scorchers!
They scream as if there were no microphones!
Let's ignore everything that was invented after Corneille!

And the way they pronounce! We better hold on tight!
They pronounce it for you from one side of the head to the other,
Without the slightest effort, like nothing at all.
"Gadzooks, everyone has to hear!"

Shouted at me one who was all dolled up just yesterday.
"I'm not the one who has your bra! It's Orestes!"
The scream is the meaning of the theater! Bunch of constipated
    jerks!
And that's nothing compared to what they do for gestures!

And they put on airs! This is art!
And art is not nothing! Bunch of acting sacks!
Big pudgy-flanked ones with the ways of a little girl
And little girls with the manners of lumberjacks!

Excuse me! Let me through! I'll show a little thigh!
Look how I speak! What extreme unction!
Imagine when I add a little force to that!
They can take away their loudspeakers, the little rascals!

Art? Phooey! Unbridled powder puffs
And little mascara types with nicotine all over their fingers!
You know, *I* get under the skin of my character!
You ought to stay there! Palmolive! Camay! False joy!34

125

Columbia settled the question of the toponymy
Of the one hundred rats, buddies of Shalac, in a snap.

One hundred rats, that's a lot, almost enough to fill up a lake.
She gave a name to each one. She's got some nerve.

One is called One, the other Two, the other Three,
And so forth one after the other. And she knows on sight
That this one is not Seventy-Four, but Thirty-One.
Only people who haven't seen anything would believe
That all rats are alike, that they all have the same face.
Each one's physiognomy is original and unique.
Fourteen has big blue eyes. Fifteen resembles Lesage.
Sixteen has a big nose. Forty is as ugly as sin.

Columbia keeps in mind what makes each one special.
She is their mother and they are her children.
This account is heartwarming like no other.
The more cootchie-cootchie-coo, the better, as far as I'm
        concerned.

In the darkness, the rats from One to One Hundred slip
Under her clothes, under her faded bodice.
Each one tries to outdo the other in sleeping closer to her heart,
Which flatters her but causes her insomnia.

She is very attached to them. But the one of whom
She is the most proud is Johann Sebastian Cur,
Her first love. But she keeps that passion secret.
She doesn't want the others to suffer like idiots because of it!

126

They encounter the Mississippi, a really well-known river.
A bridge crosses over it, but it doesn't seem any too strong.
They're hot. They're sweaty. They've run.
They'll cross in the water! They'll do sports.

The quadrupeds swim as they walk.

Those with two paws float as best they can.
The ants are carried like Noah in the ark.
The giraffe is as sad as a recent widow.

What's wrong with her? Her feet are too long for swimming.
A man cannot drown himself in a puddle.
Given her big feet, Imbecile has to ford the river.
If she had shoes on, this river wouldn't go past her teeth.
And the others laugh. Oh, how they make fun of her!
I'm not going to mention everything that they say to her.
Let us limit ourselves to noting that they chew her out with zeal.
She pretends not to hear. They'll get theirs later.

The geese and the heron are like fish in the water.
Their flippers serving as oars, they are triumphal.
Ugly on land, on the waves the heron is very handsome.
He doesn't look like a crane anymore. He looks like the swan of
    Omphale.[35]

127

Suddenly, behind the trees, they see a castle.
It is a monument so pink and so decorated with latticework
That they stop short like a thinker at the edge of the water.
They sit down on the crest of the road, more than flabbergasted.

Fingers up their noses, as serious as popes,
They admire it; they are astonished; they savor it.
One might call it a birthday cake. The tablecloth
Is the empty lawn, cut as close as velour.

Suddenly, the occupant makes his appearance.
"I see, Mademoiselle, that you are well accompanied.
Allow me to introduce myself: Néné y Obriguez y Obrégon.[36]
I have several presidencies, but my favorite

Is that of my Circle of Friends of Animals.
Come in! Come break bread in a home-style meal."
He has them eat blood pudding and lamb.
Many-colored flasks cover little tables.
He takes a picture of the group, then,
With great care, takes one of each of them.
"You are my buddies. You are my friends.
To me, each one of you is someone."
He unhooks his paintings, so that the ants can see them.
Columbia appears electrified by one all-black room
Furnished in white with a bed and a stepladder.
"That's my favorite room. It feeds my hopelessness."

128

The goose and the pachyderm keep each other company.
"I wonder where we're headed," says the more ferocious one.
"Columbia won't give us any trouble."
Are they being led to a hecatomb or to a wedding?

"I for one have complete confidence in her.
I think that she's taking us nowhere.
Columbia has been a vagabond since her childhood
And she will wander until the hour of her death.

To produce nothing is her mission."
The rhinocerotic one doesn't seem to agree.
The goose asks him a direct question.
"Do you like her a little or a lot?"

"If you really want to know: I dislike her a lot."
"C'mon, what a big liar! Hypocrite! Secretive spy!"
Because of her sore feet, Pauline-Émilienne stood up
On the head of her big companion. Go for it!

"I'm not lying. I am for liberty:

Solitude, the jungle and the rest."
Sweetie-Pie doesn't understand friendship at all.
That's what he claims. Nothing confirms it.

The goose doesn't hesitate to tell him that she loves
Their den mother as if she were made of gold.
"Just to look at her is to be baptized anew.
She cannot have failed to sweep you off your feet."

129

Abruptly, a police officer with a nose so big
That it could pass for a cape along the St. Lawrence
Applies the brakes, gets out of his all-chrome car
And addresses Columbia in a haughty and arrogant tone.

"Show me your license!" "What license, sir?"
"Do you think you can walk this menagerie around without a
        permit?
I've got news for you: you just poked yourself in the eye.
You'd better learn about law and order in the United States."

"I am Columbia Columbus," she says, in all innocence,
Smiling at him like a prostitute at a potential client.
"To drive a car, you need a license.
To drive a truck or to fly a plane too, pretty one!

Such is the reality of a democratized society.
And no one would take charge of law and order without me, the
        Police!
You are in violation or I'm still wet behind the ears,
Or I don't know my own job. So! Great!

You need four forms to walk a dog.
You don't have a single one and you're walking four of them,
        plus a heron,

Three ants, a rhinoceros, a giraffe, four felines,
Four horned beasts, four geese, a rat, a hundred baby rats.

And that's not all. You're guilty of at least hundreds of offenses."
The big old bugger-nose is ready to handcuff her.
Then the rhinoceros leaps toward him, striking him right in the
    stomach.
He flies up over the clouds. Dumbfounded, they all cry: "Holy
    crap!"

130

The gang is celebrating, jubilant; they're going wild.
What's going on? They are welcoming a new companion.
The fly found a husband along the way. That's all. That's it.
She introduces the lucky fellow to them, as Mrs. Bridges

Introduces Miss Rivers to Mr. Eagle.
Mrs. Bridges goes shopping on Fridays, around two o'clock.
Miss Rivers is indisposed during her period.
Mr. Eagle is studying harder than steel to become an ingenious
    engineer.

But one doesn't become ingenious. One is born ingenious.
And Mr. Eagle is tired of masturbating quickly all alone.
He drinks a lot of beer at night in the seedy hotel
That's not far from the big rooming house where he lives.

Ol' Ma'am Rivers goes to see the doctor, who gives her pills.
She takes them religiously. They give her arthritis.
Arthritis at her age is dreadful, the worst of ills.
Mrs. Bridges doesn't love her husband anymore. He deserves it.

When he shouts at her, she shouts louder than he. If he thinks
That she is going to let herself be imposed upon, he's got
    another thing coming.

I'd gladly cheat on him: he'd cut me up into little pieces.
When he goes out drinking, I say good riddance.

The little ones don't like all this. The oldest girl cries in her bed.
They're sensitive at that age. They don't have dry eyes.
There's got to be one who gives in, and if you're the one to give in
You're done for. Everything is lost, honor to boot.

131

Poor Columbia thinks she's dreaming!
A horse walks towards them alone!
How she's waited for it! She's going to scream.
This horse makes her holier-than-thou, prudish.

She kneels on the asphalt and
Has the others get down on their knees. Let us pray.
A white mustang, stark naked, unharnessed!
"Virgin Mary, we thank you."

They run up with open arms.
They gallop towards it.
"We are friends, solitary horse.
Come share your lot with us."

Alas, nothing gets through to it.
Under the clouds, a helicopter flies.
The handsome beast doesn't want to be tender.
"Get back, get back, you fool!"

"What's gotten into him?"
Wonder the pals, panic-stricken.
He has bitten Columbia on one shoulder,
One arm, and one hand, drawing blood.

"I am a Walt Disney star!"

He whinnies. "Look up there!
The helicopter has cameras. This is being filmed!
Pack of savages, bunch of simpletons!"

132

Poor Columbia is starting to get scared.
Five police officers have asked for her permit
Since the day before yesterday. The rhinoceros, full of ardor,
With a tremendous blow of his horns to the stomach,

Has sent each one over the clouds.
A real assault tank, that dear rhinoceros!
A real Panzer division when he's enraged.
A steamroller when he becomes ferocious.

It makes everyone laugh. It's funny.
But, alas, it's not a solution.
They'll end up doing time in the can
(A snobbish substantive signifying prison).

If you want slang, read Céline.
I am not French. *Cunt*, can't say I've ever heard of it.
If you like the Chinese, go to China.
If you're a woman, don't go there. Don't do that.

Come over to my house: I have a bit of rum left.
Come with me if you are beautiful.
And don't leave me, don't be like that
Barbara, that notorious one, that Jezebel.

Don't go to China if you're a woman.
Don't be like her. Stay with me.
Your going away will lead to a crisis.
Columbia doesn't know what to do. To each his cross to bear.

133

For the permit, Pauline-Émilienne, the goose,
Has found a sort of answer, a kind of solution.
Every animal breeder has one of them. That goes without saying.
Here it is: the goose – the dirty dog – has the firm intention

Of stepping through the door of the first breeder
They meet and of committing a holdup there!
With Columbia's revolver she won't be afraid.
"Hand zap! It's thieves like me who take the rap!

The loners! No union, no vacation.
We don't have two pleasant weeks per year,
Because we don't give pennies monthly.
Give me your permit, venerable breeder!"

Roguish, Pauline-Émilienne imagines the pained expression
That the man will have when she tells him all that.
He'll quake in his boots: "Have pity on me, goose! Mercy!"
The (slightly) volatile one, waddling, projects what will happen

After she's spied a farm, a tractor in the distance.
When she waves the gun under the guy's nose,
He'll lose all his spunk. He'll change his tune.
He'll become yellow and then green.

Waddling by the layer of asphalt, she laughs
Under her breath. The sky is blue. The sun is enchanting.
The road is endless. How beautiful life is!
"Mr. Breeder, the papers! Or else I'll be mean!"

134

Columbia and the animals are in quite a state.
Mysteriously, the goose has flown the coop.
"There! Over there!" shouts Bic. "In the tobacco field!

That white form with yellowy orange spots!

Alas, what the ant has seen is not Pauline-Émilienne.
"That's not her, you idiot! That's a twister!"
"What's that? Does it look like her offspring?"
"Where have you been? Good grief! Don't you know your own
    sister?"

Bic, the ant, doesn't know what a twister is.
Each time she thinks that she's seen Pauline-Émilienne,
They tell her: "That's not her, you idiot! That's a twister!"
And they ask her if, by chance, she might not be from Mars.

Poor Columbia cries like Mary Magdalene.
They do everything they can to console her.
The dogs lick her. The rats give her a full inkwell:
They just found it at the foot of a big notebook.

The heron catches a blue-winged dragonfly.
Instead of eating it, he gives it to her, saying in his fluty voice:
"It's an animal like us." They do their best.
She'll never forget the goose who, trumpeting,

Was wandering far ahead of them for more than a month.
She says to the fly: "Do you know the language of dragonflies?"
"Yes, and I'll do everything to integrate her into our environment."
Her iridescent wings are as light as tulle.

135

Four days go by without news of Pauline-Émilienne.
It's raining cats and dogs. Charleston is in sight.
"Mama!" The little goslings[37] cry and thrash about.
Almost everyone considers the goose to be lost.

But Bic has not abandoned her observation post:

The end of the giraffe's longest horn.
"I hear trumpet calls on the horizon!"
"Trumped again! You're wrong; those are bang-bangs."

But the insect is sure of her discovery this time.
"I swear to you; I heard and I hear trumpet calls."
"O.K.! Sure! Enough! That's fine! We believe you!
You'll tell us when you hear a scooter beep!"
"Don't make fun of her!" commands Columbia severely.
"That poor little dear is doing her best!"
In addition to the goose's loud honk, Bic, now,
Hears growling, yapping. Indescribable sounds burst forth!

She isn't dreaming: she has heard a neigh.
If only it weren't raining, too. You can't see anything
Through a curtain of drops multiplied by a hundred.
The rain ceases. She sees as though in a mirror.

What clarity! Running faster than she's able, followed
By a horse, six hogs, fifteen cows, sixteen roosters and two dogs,
Pauline-Émilienne, opening her wings to her friends,
Cries out: "At last! At last! At last! At last! At last!"

136

The wheat has just been harvested. So many stacks of straw!
Columbia lights one of them up. They huddle close to the fire.
"While we're warming up, tell us of your battles."
They listen to the wet goose as closely as they can.

"I go into the old bachelor's dirty house.
He's in the middle of dinner. I aim my weapon. He raises his hands.
Give me your permit or I'll kill you, assassinate you, just like that.
He swells up, explodes. He collapses: he's done for.

I suppose he was a dreadfully cardiac case.

I search everywhere. No way to find the permit.
Outside, the cows are grazing, the hogs are playing in the puddles;
Standing up, the roosters cock-a-doodle-do vehemently.

What's going to become of them without a breeder?
What's going to become of these cows? Their tits are going to
    explode!
Truly, I was pierced to the heart by it.
So, I trumpet, I make some conversation.

I, old pals, have a mistress as beautiful as a heart.
They say, 'Really?' Of course it's true.
And she's so good she'll knock your socks off.
They say, 'Really?' If you came, you'd see.

I open the doors and the gates. Let's go!
The road was too long! They wanted to lynch me,
Sort of the way the sailors wanted to drown Columbus.
They thought that I had told them untruths.
Where are your buddies, your lovely mistress? I almost died."

137

The cow and the calves smell the cows.
The dogs smell the new dogs.
They all have to get to know one another, to no one another.
It's their way of bonding.

They inform themselves, quietly, exchanging taps on the muzzle.
"What sex are you? Are you as strong as you seem?"
When fights threaten to break out, Columbia shouts: "Oh!"
Columbia uses her most severe tone.

"Enough! What's gotten into you, naughty one?
Do you have an inferiority complex or what?
There's only room here for hugs!

Just let me catch you at it again, you little cad of dubious repute!"

Dubious repute is not used in that sense.
I know it. Go tell that to Columbia Columbus!
She'll tell you where you can put your fix-that-for-me!
She'll make you swallow your grammar, you lousy no-show!

"So many of them to meet!" sighs Fic.
The new arrivals only see her and her sisters when they
Have the ants in their eyes. And that shuts them right up.
"They make as much room for these minis as for me?" they say.

The dragonfly lands on the snout of one of the hogs.
He's getting ready to give her a good swift kick.
"Pals like pigs?" "Well, I never!"
"I'm biting you? Don't worry, just scratch."

138
"Every rooster has its Spain. It is under their feathers."
That's by Nikolai Gogol, in *Diary of a Madman*.
Poor Columbia, who has caught a bad cold,
Wonders whether it's true. She questions a red rooster.

"It's the pure truth!" he answers her, quite astonished.
"That devilish Russian writer should have held his tongue!"
"The one who should have held his tongue," says the girl with
    the cold,
"Isn't it rather the rooster who told it to him, proud Brung?"

Brung is the name of the cock with whom she's chatting.
Sixteen cocks: sixteen Spains! No wonder the hens lay eggs!
She'd like to see the Iberia that the feathers mask.
Brung says yes. He shows it to her in silence, without
    loquaciousness.

Under the abundant red feathers she can see a Spain,
A hundred times more clearly than in a big atlas.
So many olives! She sees it as well as one would see Tarzan's
  rear end,
If he were to take off his loincloth. Flamenco all over!

"Don't tell anyone!" crows Brung to her sternly.
"Swear it! I don't want any ifs, ands or buts!
I require a vow in the name of the cocks here in attendance!"
She says: "You can count on me! I promise!"

"We aren't tight-fisted," he goes on, softening.
"Whenever a Spain is useful to you, you have only to say so.
For you and your friends, there will always be in us, plentifully,
The wherewithal to do everything in our power to please."

139

She is very glad to have a horse.
Her passion for horses is well known.
She'll never give him a hard time.
She won't sit on his back like a jockey.

She will treat this animal, the sight of which
Inflames her soul to the point at which
Sparks fly from her eyes, as if she were a lady
And he were a man come from on high.

He is beautiful. She will let him be beautiful.
And that's all that she will let him do.
She will not harness him. Far from it!
He will walk next to her, like a brother.

She loves his hooves, hard as teeth,
And will always love them.
His breath, hot as blood,

Will be to her cheek what the sun is to flowers.

She will seek to imitate, to equal his gait,
Light and ever so elegant.
His velvety forehead still tempts
The palm that just feasted upon it.

She feels the slenderness and the excitability
Of his forelegs and hind legs already in her legs.
Her Catherine the Great side stuns you.
If he dies, she will be far from happy. Let's not doubt it for an
    instant.

140

Those who usually want to put her in prison,
Under the pretext that she has no permit to show,
Seem to be the highway patrolmen.
Their appearance is that of any good highway cop.

But often things aren't so clear.
Indeed, here comes one of those so-called officers.
Before the rhinoceros makes his day,
Launches him as a maple bow would a pine arrow,

They're going to try to verify his authenticity.
Columbia makes him believe that she's turning herself in.
"I've given the order to my rhinoceros not to attack.
I've done enough harm. I'm holding out my wrists for your
    handcuffs."

"Young lady, it is too late but there is still time.
You do realize that you may get the chair.
Ah! My supervisors will be so happy!
I am proud of myself! Now I can breathe easy."

He's boasting, relaxing. He feels safe.
The time has come! To blind him, the dragonfly and the flies
Throw themselves into his eyes. Everyone jumps him from all
      sides.
They throw him down, hit him, bite him, lay him out.

"Shut your trap!" He's shouting, tied to the ground.
Columbia takes off his caca-green uniform,
Pulls off his lovely shirt, removes his pretty undershirt.
On the hairy torso shines the cross of the union of unions!

141

Along the side of the road, between Augusta and another town,
There are many groups of black human beings.
Columbia gets on well with them and opens up her heart to a
      thousand.
Alas, she falls in with some extremists. They show her a thing
      or two!

"We can't swallow the fact that you're the color of doves,
That your nose is whiter than the inside of your hand!"
When they get started, they're meaner than bombs!
She endures while saying to herself: "We really deserve it!"

They throw big pom-poms right in her nose.
"Will you look at that! It's as white as a cigarette!"
They slam her with pieces of New Guinea!
"She doesn't even have breasts big enough for lice to suckle!"

If the animals weren't there as a rampart,
To intercept all the big things that they're firing off,
She would be lifeless or, at the very least, somewhere
Between life and death. "And music? Dance?

What color is it if it isn't black?

If you don't want to give us the right to rub elbows
With you in busses, trains and on the sidewalks,
We will lynch you. And when do we get the right to vote?"

They reproach her for having put Rome and Athens in her past,
And for having put nothing but bananas and coconuts in their
    history.
"Repent now or we won't let you pass!"
"You're mistaken!" She suffers. What must be must be.

142

Farther on, in the vicinity of Blackville,
Something almost incredible happens to them.
For fear of being called an idiot, a simpleton, an imbecile,
I feel like passing over this frightful turn of events.

Begging the reader's indulgence, the author carries on.
On the road, in the middle, sits imposingly a large pewter cylinder.
"That can cause some unprecedented accidents!"
Who yapped that? It's Johann Sebastian Bark!

He runs to clear the road. "What an object!"
He examines the cylinder curiously.
At one end, a lens is visible. "What's this?"
At the other end, and this is the most fearful of all,

It displays and brandishes a contraption similar to
What is left of a horse's tail after it has been cut.
Suddenly, the object expands to enormous size
And hits the dog, hurting him more than a sword!

"SOS! Run for your life! It's a living telescope!"
Getting longer in unexpected ways, the living instrument,
Like a battering ram, hits the mamas, hits the children,
Hits Columbia, the giraffe, the fly, the ants!

It's as though it had the intention of sparing no one;
It stretches out sharply, and draws itself in suddenly.
It's aimed like a canon! Sweetie-Pie kills it with a blow of his
    horns.
A dirty trick by the unions, probably. How crafty!

143

They're getting closer and closer to Charleston.
Will they ever get there?
"Fifty miles!" said a bearded man to them.
Columbia has many wounds to bandage.

The biggest wound belongs to Imbecile, the giraffe.
That's not a play on words. One of his femurs is broken.
And that's a bone as big as a telephone pole.
Columbia is in quite a predicament, up to her ears in work.

Tying splints to the leg of a herbivorous
Mammal like that is too much for her little arms.
She feels like crying, like packing it all in.
"My God, help me! Capone, don't forsake me!"

Fortunately, lying on her flank, her eyes closed,
The giraffe is as calm as a chocolate bunny.
And the rhinoceros, the longtime companion, her best-beloved,
Looking on sternly all the while! "Don't you go getting the big
    idea,"

He seems to say, "of operating on her the wrong way.
And above all, don't make her suffer!
If I hear her screaming as if on a cross,
Don't go making any long-term plans."

And Vic's joint between the thorax and the abdomen is cracked!
And the other one's skull is split right down his face!

A thousand cuts, the size of hazelnuts! Oh! She wants to get out
    of there!
Serving as a doctor is no sinecure!

144

By dint of patience, Columbia has taught Cur her language.
He is bilingual: he yaps and speaks. How sweet it is!
Now, they can talk together without beating about the bush,
Like two white Russians from Orel or Ivanovo!

"Are you doing better, my dear?" she asks him.
"I'm fine, Columbia. I'm great. Couldn't be better," he replies.
"What a telescope! In the future, watch out for ladders.
There might even be retractable ones.

What will they think of next!" "Huh?"
"I said that perhaps they've invented living ladders."
His head mummified, the dog smiles as poorly as could be
    expected.
"Without mishaps, life would be boring."

"Those confounded unions, honestly!" says Columbia.
Since more or less all of them are limping, they don't make
    much progress.
They say that the unions are more deadly than bombs.
Johann Sebastian is thinking about what is stirring in his belly.

Animals are perverted; all they think about is mating.
"Columbia, I'm going to have puppies again."
"Well! Well! Just who is threatening to overpopulate the earth?
It wouldn't be a certain Johann Sebastian?"

"I'm not the only one. The goose is also going to give birth soon.
And three of the hog's bodies are so swollen that they may
    explode.

Several rats and the fly have pretty big bellies."
Columbia's heart races as if she were breathless.

145

Johann Sebastian ought to be called Joanne Sebastianne.
I know, I know! And the fly Quadrimotor
Ought to be called Quadrimotrice or "Good-for-Nazis."
(That's the feminine form of "good-for-nothings.") I know, dear
    reader.

It's poor dear Columbia who doesn't know.
What do you expect? She doesn't associate with gynecologists.
She's not like you. She's not like that.
When an animal is given to her, zebra or bulldog,

She doesn't push aside its tail to look at its rear end.
No! She is not of the race of those who do that!
She knows full well that Johann Sebastian is a mother, not a father.
But feminine, masculine, for her, is all blablabla.

Everyone has such a scientific attitude! I'm gnashing my teeth!
It's just that a dog, to her, always has a boy's face.
Does one say she or he of an assertive papa "fly," a feminine word?
Does one say she or he of a dirty-minded papa "giraffe," a
    feminine word?

Whatever you may think, Columbia doesn't have any sexual
    problems.
She is not fair game for the psychoanalyst's couch.
Our beautiful Russian language is badly made. Too bad for her!
As for the colonialist paper tigers,

They have nothing to do with this, although, like bombs,
One has a tendency to serve them with every dish.
Why did I have to fall into a world like this?

I've wanted to commit suicide for a pretty long time: here I go!

146

Bic the ant asks Pauline-Émilienne the goose:
"When, my dearest, will you give birth?"
"You're sliding down a slippery slope. I'm not a female dog.
Geese lay eggs and sit on them. I'm ovoviviparous, you see.

And an ant, if I am not mistaken, is ovipositor."
Well, now! Here goes Pauline-Émilienne getting into the act, too.
Telling an ant how she brings her children into the darkness!
Ovipositor! Ovipositor, yourself! How coarse! Get lost!

147

That night, a stone's throw from Charleston or maybe two,
Pauline gave birth, then two of the hogs did, then Quadrimotor,
Then Two, Three, Seven, Twenty, Thirty, Thirty-three,
Seventy, Twelve and Seventeen. What happiness!

In order to give birth, for the surprise, they go hide.
When everything is OK, they call: "Come see!"
Columbia and the others were not able to remain in bed
For more than two minutes at a time that night.

The fathers are not all present. Those who are
Distribute cigars. "Columbia!" says Bic, the ant,
Appearing suddenly on the end of her nose. "You were startled.
I took you by surprise, huh? You were caught unawares.

Columbia, don't you ever ever give birth?"
This question pierces her heart and disarms her.
A vagina that is useless, how sad, my goodness!
She is very surprised by the power of the charm

That the ant's interrogation has over her heart.
"Let's make a deal," says Bic. "I'll be the papa, and you, the
        mama."
"The papa and the mama of what?" "Why, of our little ones."
"Tell me the whole story!" says Columbia, taking the matter
        patiently.

"I deposit my eggs deep down in your hair. Two days!
After that, they break open, and it's wriggle and wail galore!"
Columbia tells Bic to stop flirting with her.
Deep down, she'd like him to be able to be her lover.

148
"We'll never get to Charleston if this keeps up."
So that those who have given birth may rest,
They have interrupted their big, beautiful trip.
They haven't moved for three or four days.

Columbia has had little ants. They are doing well.
Their mother too, thank you. They run through her hair,
Like Indian warriors between pines and firs.
They look like their papa. Believe it if you will.

There are so many, so very many newcomers to the group
That the Carolina autumn is all decked out as spring.
Autumn has to be decked out as autumn or face a fine.
The weather's beautiful. Everyone's comfortable. It's tremendous.

So? My metaphors? They fail to please? You may simply leave.
Besides, my semaphores are even worse.
A third hog, at the last minute, has decided
That he too will surprise them. Someone has said,

"We'll never get to Charleston if this keeps up."

Columbia, one can well imagine, has scolded the author of those
    words.
"Who do you think you are, you worthless little pipsqueak?
You must be polite. You should have gone to school."
Charleston is there, in the ocean mist.
The little ants are there, in her blond hair,
In her hair so long, so fine, so shiny.
Despite the autumn, flowers thrive in every eye.

149

No concrete in Charleston; it's all wood.
Hotels, banks, sidewalks and houses are made of wood.
The lucky ones who have been there know it!
The local yokels, just like you and me, are made of crud.

But they still make wooden faces at the newcomers,
Like anywhere else. Of course, you don't have to be really smart
To smile when you see a giraffe nibbling on your flowers.
No reason to go overboard. It's pretty clear.

For Imbecile, who can jump over fences with his neck,
Charleston is a delight, a real feast, an orgy.
Charleston is a small city where the growing
Of garden flowers has a place of honor. You don't think so? Go
    see for yourself!

All at once, they find themselves in front of a cement block.
A little man made up of oxidized copper is standing on it.
His sword gives him a hot-blooded air.
Pigeons, it goes without saying, have pooped on him.

"Billy Willy fondled (founded?) Charleston in the year one
    thousand.
When he died, he was mourned by all.
Does a city more beautiful than Charleston exist?

No!" The Americans spend their time boasting.

A squirrel gazes at itself in the golden plaque where that is written.
Columbia is not impressed by that founder's statue.
You get used to those things, those matters,
When you've spent your whole childhood with a discoverer.

150

Suddenly, they have the chance to go to the opera.
The gallinacean incarnating Cock-a-doodle-doo has died and
    the director
Asks the group to lend him a rooster with a voice.
"We must be admitted without paying, as spectators."

They are given, forthwith, a hundred of the best seats.
On the program: *The Purchased Bride* by the great Smetana.[38]
They are seated. It starts in a few hours.
There is a photo of Sibelius,[39] but not of Smetana,

In the dictionary that Columbia has.
Ah! If only the great Smetana knew that!
The tiers are filling up with knaves.
The rats, stricken with fear, twenty by twenty,

Come throw themselves on Columbia. "What are those?"
Asks a man sitting next to her.
She's got them up to her glasses. "They're rats, of course!"
"For the operata, my dear young lady?"

Three hammer blows are heard. A bit of scenery
Had come loose, probably. Suddenly, the curtain rises and rustles.
The stage is a room full of multicolored drapes.
Cock-a-doodle-doo's costume is quite becoming on their
    rooster. They applaud.

Do tenors and basses eat until they burst?
The female singers are enormous as well. What arms!
As big as normal people's thighs! As if they were bloated.
Columbia thinks: "They really take care of themselves in those
    circles!"
And she used to think that artists were as thin as rakes.

151

The opera *The Purchased Bride* by the great Smetana
Has the curiosity of staging a stutterer.
I can't help it. That's life. That's how it is.
True to the author, the baritone, from the top of his breeches,

Sings with a stutter. Columbia and the others explode.
Holding their stomachs, they laugh like hyenas.
Those who think the opera is God turn scarlet.
"Oh! My handkerchief! Oh! My heart! Oh! The little rascals!"

As covered by tears of laughter as by rats, Columbia
Asks the gentleman seated on the right if it's a mistake.
"Is he stuttering on purpose…?" She succumbs.
She's laughing so hard she can't continue. A Miss Take?

"Or is it that he's an out-of-tuna barrel-of-tuna who stutters in
    daily life?"
Infected by her laughter, the man replies almost this:
"Ha ha ha ha ho ho… he's stuttering on purpose. You're so funny!
Stop! Stop! Ho ho ho ho ho ha ha ha ha ha ha…"

The pleasure of humor lasts but for a moment. "What are you
    doing there?"
The Union of Infectious-Laugh-Squelchers-at-the-Opera[40]
(Union affiliated with the Union of Those in Stitches[41])
Has turned up in the form of a henchman,

Has made its appearance, in the person of a policeman.
He's a big Irishman armed to the teeth.
Human beings armed like that are to be discouraged,
Even if, on television, they distract children.

152

They end up on a quay,
Just above the ocean.
Where to go from here?
Now which way does the wind blow?

The water clearly precludes the east.
Will they take the south or the north?
They watch the busy seagulls,
Who cry out there and here.

It's so cold their teeth are chattering.
If only they could fly!
Onward to the east! Full steam ahead!
If only they could walk on water!

Under the quay, there's not much room.
In order to sleep, they settle in.
In order to sleep, they cram in.
They feast on each other.

They caress one another, some until midnight.
Each one is more loving than the twelve apostles.
Snuggle up to me, my sister, my friend.
Columbia thinks of Manna and of Wother.

Tomorrow, she will make a decision.
Torn apart by the compass card,
Rooted to the spot in all four directions,
She won't sleep for long.

153

If only they could fly. Even on a broomstick!
There would be no Atlantic big enough, deserted enough, deep
    enough!
If she were alone, she would cross it swimming.
Over there, not very far, so close that its name

Is legible to those who have good eyes,
Floats a deluxe ocean liner belonging to the Cunard company.
If only they could fly! That's it! My God!
Why didn't she think of it sooner? What an idiot!

She speaks to the rooster boss, dubbed Big Belly.
"You see that boat over there? Could you fly to it?"
"My dear, roosters fly badly. Let me think about it...
I know one named Louis who boasts that he can outrun the rain."

Louis has the waist of a swallow and the wings of a vulture.
"I'm the best-flying rooster in the U.S.!"
"Can you fly all the way to that boat? You'd be such a dear!..."
In a frightening way, he beats his wings. He has blushed!

A huge crowd gathers right away.
"Louis has Spain under his wings. It's a big country:
506,787 km2, not counting the Balearic and Canary Islands.
We could bring Portugal along with us on Louis."
Once he is on the boat, he'll crow three times.

Not to mention that they will let him land
As if he were a mere seagull.
The albatrosses on the boat are not inconvenienced.
Well? Are we ready? We're off! Hurray for the big thinkers!

154

Seated on the edge of Madrid, they wait.
They hear the agreed-upon crows as a signal.
They leave the warm grass of an almond garden.
They find themselves at the foot of a naval battleship.

From far away, the boat looked gray.
It is red, Pravda red, a stifling red.
"My God! The ants! Where are the ants?"
They look at each other, their mouths solemn, their eyes round.

Softly, alarmed, Columbia fingers her hair.
Not only the adults, but also the children are missing.
"What's happened to Sic, Cic and Zic, my God?"
If she were Roland, she would sound the ivory horn.

155

This wretched red liner
Is registered at Angra, capital of the Azores,
An archipelago which is anchored and which, sometimes, moves
In the middle of waves where several sailors have died.

Now, it is going back home. Which means,
If I have clearly understood, that they will end up stuck
Right in the middle of the Atlantic if
They let this liner named Pootertobed do what it wants.

In other words, they must not have complete
Confidence in this tourist-exporting ocean liner
If they want, as indeed they do desire,
Not to have a sad stay on some islands.

They are still without news from the ants.
Why the hell did they leave the group?
What does the Pootertobed crew look like?

It's not too large. It's rather small.

In other words, it comes down to this:
If Columbia and the animals wanted to, they could, yes,
They could, easily, with three or four guns,
Take over the ocean liner and make it their taxi.

Taxis are used to move people from one place to another.
I thus have employed the word taxi quite advisedly.
Ladies, young ladies (hmmm!) and gentlemen,
Do appreciate the extent of my knowledge and the brilliance of
   my talent!

156

Properly, gently, without killing, without even injuring anyone,
They have taken over the helm of the red ocean liner.
The rats took care of the captain. They slipped
Under his covers. "What's this? What's moving?"

Put yourself in his place. Imagine one hundred thirty rodents
In your bed, on your neck, on your back,
Down your legs, over your heart.
He threw himself overboard. Let's hope that a raft,

One of these days, will come, will be at his disposal.
When, suddenly, they noticed that they were right
Under the eyes of a giraffe, the boiler room guys
Rolled their eyes and shouted, "It can't be!"

And they lost consciousness, fainted right away.
When they saw a dragonfly pointing a gun
In their direction, the cooks laughed.
When the dragonfly shot the gun, they cried out

And they too, all at once, lost consciousness.

As for the one who, in the books that I can't stand,
Holds on to the mast like a monkey to take note
Of what's happening north, south, east and west,

As for that one, I say, he fell straight down
From his perch when he saw two armed flies
Land on his big nose, shiny as a mirror.
Columbia is proclaimed Pope of the Battleship.

157

The ants have not given any sign of life.
The others just can't get used to their absence.
Truly, their disappearance makes them want
To cry immense tears every day.

The sword that this disappearance has thrust into their hearts
Has left a wound that will never heal again.
This tragedy has rendered the sweetness
That births give them even sweeter than before May.

By that, I mean that each time that in the group
Another being is born, they are more grateful
Than they had been before their hearts were broken,
Before the discovery of the absence of the ants and of their
        children.

When it's not clear enough, say so. Don't be shy.
Suddenly, an albatross falls at their feet, unconscious.
What joy on the bridge, under the blazing sun!
Far from putrid are the fish that, making haste,

They feed to the great white bird
That looks more like a gull than a lark.
It drags itself along the iron girder, miserably rowing
With its wings, too long to flap. "The poor harpy!"

They pity it. It could only fly
If it were to perch upon stilts! It cannot take off.
Ask Baudelaire. He'll go on and on for you.
And in alexandrines, no less! It's all the more pitiful that way.[42]

158

The ocean liner slices through the water like all boats.
The shore has not yet been sighted,
Has not yet put in an appearance. "Hello! Hello!"
They shout to the old porpoises which swim

Around the hull the way vultures
Fly above a zebra carcass.
Pootertobed is going adrift. Go ahead, my love!
Take us where you will! They have thrown overboard the compass,

A dismal instrument, to be disputed by sharks.
Take us where you will, dear red liner!
They have broken the rudder, have stuffed it into a corner.
Is it taking them to Denmark, land of Eric the Red?

Is it taking them to Ghana, which has conquered its freedom?
Will they be washed up onto a beach of the South African
     Republic?
The Cunard hides a secret between its rusty sides.
Will they arrive in a little while or next year?

They've solved the albatross's problem with a stepladder.
There's nothing but fish left on the menu.
The sun rises and sets from stem to stern.
In all of her glory, unveiled, stark naked,

In order to take in everything that happens night and day,
Columbia, the rover, spends her time sleeping
On the tarred roof of the almost rosy transatlantic liner.

The albatross can't decide. Will he spend his future with them?

159

They are proud, glad. The albatross is coming along.
Instead of fish, they swallow bananas.
Joyously, they're walking in the middle of Mauritania.
They're walking as if they'll never stop. The ocean breeze,

Now, is way back there, far behind.
They've eaten up all the ocean sun.
They've drunk the ocean darkness, down to its last drop,
Like a thimble of orange-tree water.

Now, they're stuffing their faces with jungle.
They're up to here with tigers and tigresses.
And the Negroes, biting their nails,
Look out from the backwaters in distress,

While you, you can't quite swallow these pages.
Everyone is always consuming something.
My mouth is glued shut from not being able to munch on your face;
I'm going crazy waiting for you,

I who know not Hutu love,
Nor if I would find love as I wander in Rwanda.
Never mind, perhaps I'll see you here,
A girl sitting on my bed, the bed of a penitent monk.

160

Dear readers, remember in your prayers
That I am telling you the beautiful story of Columbia
        Columbus,
A globe-trotter with glasses saying her prayers every night,
Pin-up too, holder of a unique pair of tits.

This beautiful story, believe it or not, was lived.
It was imposed on me like a past by something
That I have in my head but that I don't hear anymore,
By some kind of inevitable sun, black and pink.

Everything that I touch I botch.
The pink, when I apply it, is mixed with gray.
My black is brown like cow dung.
But I'll go on until the end: I have spoken.

If I were less nauseated by life,
I would probably tell you this beautiful story better.
When one feels like committing suicide, my dear,
The verse gets worse and bursts as you go along.

161

Long live May 17, 1966! Yes, sir!
The dockers of Montreal, Quebec, and Trois-Rivières are on strike.
Their parking lots are too muddy for their Cadillacs.
The sailors of Great Britain or else of England
Are on strike. They want fewer hours and more pay.

Seven million French are on strike.
The Greyhound busses of California, Nevada,
Arizona, Utah and eight other States of the western
United States are on strike.

They want more pay.
That disgusts me. I don't know why.
It makes me wish I were dead.
The newspapers of New York, Boston, Baltimore and others
Are on strike. They want more pay.

God, what hole have you put me in?
God, what kind of a mess is this?

God, is there no one here but capitalists
And communists?
God, you've put me in with a bunch of bellyachers, money
    collectors,
Slogan-slobberers and shitty placard-holders!
God, are they really that heartless and unimaginative?
God, how they disgust me!
And the men (or women) write to Ann Landers to say
That their wives (their husbands) are not dirty-minded
Enough.
And their sons let their hair grow to look like the Beatles!

162

Indeed, some joyous strikers have just gone by,
Under my sad windows. Big grins running ear to ear,
Their rear ends on a red padded seat in a late-model Chevrolet,
A late-model Pontiac or a late-model

Ford convertible, they seemed
To be part of the St. John the Baptist Midsummer's Day parade.
They were honking like mad, big grins running ear to ear.
"Down with Dominion Textile!" "Reasonable salaries!"
"We'll die penniless!" "We're hungry!"

Could one, could I read in green on the white cards
That were plastered on their automobiles, on the white cards
That they brandished joyously through the windows of their
1966 model automobiles.

The other day, in front of the Hydro-Quebec building,
There were engineers and engine-ears who were pacing
Back and forth (you have to believe that they knew how to walk)
With union signs in their hands. They looked like
Choir boys and girls

Participating in the Corpus Christi procession.
They were carrying the placards in the same way that
Choir girls and boys carry the banners in the Corpus Christi
Procession in Spain.
And I thought that engineers and engine-ears had
Nothing to learn from choir boys and girls.
More fascist than the Church!

163

They forge the path they follow as they go.
Oh! It's so good! How they love it!
In this Mauritanian desert, the Fez-Ur desert,
There just aren't any roads or footpaths.

The African deserts are authentic deserts.
Nothing grows there, nothing, absolutely nothing.
In America, the deserts are almost green.
Sage grows there in great quantities. Those Americans!

They walk, dashing right toward the Levant.
Walking is good for one's health. Radiant are the walkers!
For snobs: jogging is stupendous.
They just do without water. Drinkers are despicable!

They ought to have no way to get a bite to eat.
What do they eat? They eat sand and prize it.
How can you croak in a place full of such nourishment?
For it is indeed nourishment! At least that's what they tell each
    other.
You have to look at the sand's good side.
You have to have a hardy constitution.
Believe me, I find nothing more gauche
Than someone who grimaces and gets angry when,

Instead of blood-pudding, he finds siliceous soil on his plate.

Human beings, who sweat to cultivate Chinese cabbage,
Must be stupid enough to eat hay for not having thought
Of harvesting the sand, that fruit of millions of years of nothing!

164
There, at the very edge of the horizon,
The desert is turning red as if it were imbibing wine.
What can it be? It's not a mirage, for
In animals illusions do not hold sway.

What is it? They try hard to understand.
It's getting red quickly! The entire countryside
Has changed color, and it's not just a decor:
It's advancing like the shadow of an immense cloud.

What kind of blood-red simoom will they be caught in?
It's alive! They've been convinced of it for a little while.
It's worse, for they hear loads of tiny sounds,
Like those of a million fly legs on something soft.

They think of the Bible. It's an invasion of locusts!
If it is one, well then! So much the better; they'll have a
    delightful time.
One must not fear for one's life, or collapse like loose string!
When you're solid, you can look on the bright side every time.

What do they see, separating itself from the banks of the
    vermilion mass,
And running faster than a wolf while calling their names?
It's Bic! They run to meet him, hug him.
"We went to get all the ants. It took a long time!"

165

Sic, Cic and Zic have again taken up residence deep
In the blond hair of their magnificent mama.
Billions of ants, ants by the millions
Spread around them like a vast layer of blood.

It can't be said that Columbia is not proud.
Her eyes and heart are no longer big enough.
All the ants, the whole world's ants,
Are given to her like a letter to the mail carrier!

She's dripping with sweat! Her dress sticks to her skin.
Seated on her nose, his anterior legs crossed, Bic explains himself.
"It was jealousy that made me act like a fool.
It's because of Shalac. He's the one who took the wind out of
      my sails.

I never told anyone, but I became
Green with shame, envy and jealousy when that old rat
Came back with a hundred of his kind. How you welcomed them!
I had never seen you more moved than that!

I promised myself to one-up him. Do you understand it all now?"
Columbia has understood everything. She is very intelligent.
She's not stupid, not an imbecile like you!
I'd bet my future fortune that you didn't get it!

Bic, quite simply, wanted to create a surprise
Bigger and better than that which Shalac gave her
By bringing her a hundred of his buddies. OK, dear Liza?
If you haven't grasped that, you deserve to be sacked.

166

Since they're at the foot of the Pyramids, they make the most of
    it by drinking,
For the first time in weeks, some Aitch-too-oh.
It was about time that all that sweat poured out
By thousands of black Egyptians, in order to erect
Those tremendous funeral bungalows, be used for something.
Don't you think so, Jane Doe? You don't, Joe Shmoe?

167

A thin lion and tiger have smelled human flesh.
They approach the sleeping Columbia, stealthy as wolves.
The lucky stiffs are drooling so much, they're out of breath.
They don't suspect that the rover with such a sweet stench

Is not lying alone in her unceremonious gown,
Is not sleeping alone in her dirty and torn cotton dress.
If they had the slightest idea of the number of fat rats
That are dreaming like hunting dogs on her pearly skin,

They would be off and running.
They skirt way around the rhinoceros. Prudence
Is the mother of security. Bold they are, and crazy!
Having jumped over all the ants of France

(There aren't that many but they're not without volubility),
They land within an inch of their gracious victim.
To whet their appetites, they wait for a few seconds.
Eating is not murder. Hunger is no crime.

The rats are only half asleep. Through the holes in the bodice,
They've seen almost everything. All together they throw
    themselves,
Abruptly, upon the two anthropophagous marauders.
They bite with gusto. When rats get started,

They do more than just nibble, please believe me!
Through a thousand holes the blood spurts forth, out of the eyes,
      the ears.
Columbia, awake, can't stand the sight of them.
To calm them down, she clouts them with a bottle.

168

With a needle and thread, Columbia sews up
The torn skin of the lion and tiger, still in a coma.
The rats themselves also were quite beaten up.
Bruises are puffing up all over their bodies.

"They are animals too, you crazy rats!"
Columbia is angry. The rats nearly murdered them.
"You would do better to keep a low profile
If you don't want to have a few more

Beer-bottle blows doled out to you!"
The animals, grouped around her like houses
Around old-fashioned churches made of stone,
Are astonished that that she favors the mean ones.

169

The lion and the tiger are greatly feared.
Not being cordial, they are judged to be deceitful.
The cows tremble when they come to suckle.
The flies have lost their appetites. As for the geese,

They say: "We can't even close our eyes for an instant."
The lion and the tiger communicate with no one.
They walk side by side, far away, chewing on one leaf or
      another,
If not on some infernal plan, some diabolical idea.

It's amazing that Columbia is still alive,
That she has been spared by the king of the animals and by the
     prince.
The trip has become an unbearable wait.
Her chances of longevity are held to be so slim

That some speak in low tones about going back home.
Let that morning come when they'll find nothing
But her bones! They say that it's better, my goodness,
That she be devoured right away. They can't stand it any longer!

They're tired of trembling, of worrying themselves sick.
Does she think that a lion and a tiger will long be happy
Living on cow's milk and on this salt that is sand?
They have the impression that they're being led by a latent corpse.

The two predators will eat Columbia. Then they will lick their
     chops.
At night, some of the others cry out in pain.
In their dreams, their den mother so beautiful, so sweet, so fine,
Is devoured several times, always by the same two.

170

Let's talk again about that tiger and that lion.
Despite Columbia's interdiction, they caught a jackal
And they ate it, savored it from bottom to top.
It can no longer be saved by any hospital.

Its tongue smeared with blood, the lion,
Proud of its triumph, licked the rover's face.
The tiger, its paws wet, leapt and
Swooped down on her joyously from behind,

Making her fall flat on the ground.

Columbia is giving up hope of getting them to understand
    anything.
She forgives them. Toward them too she feels maternal.
Do they lack kindness? Are they merely a little childish?

"A jackal is an animal, like you."
The others look on, with a discouraged air.
They are drunk with worry, reeling with anxiety.
Things don't seem to be likely to work out.

The Red Sea is closer and closer to them.
"It's like a strait; we'll cross it swimming!"
They ask heaven and the good Lord
To have the big cats drown round the bend.

171

To shame the mean tiger and the nasty lion,
Columbia and the others hold a grandiose funeral for the jackal.
The little casket has handles in the shape of violins.
The hearse, black, shining like a general's boots,

Is pulled by an ox covered with big blue flowers.
Ants by the millions take out their handkerchiefs.
The others too. "Victim of a heinous crime!"
One can read on the sash of a crown of black tulips.

Chased away by Columbia, the two murderers, seated on a dune,
Wait for it to finish, trying vaguely to understand.
The sun rises. The sun sets. In the moonlight,
The funeral service continues. "We ought to hang them!"

Yap the dogs to the tune of *A Star Is Fallen*.
Columbia, her face awash with tears, throws the first shovelful
On the coffin, which contains only a few hairs.
She does as she did at the funeral of her father, poisoned to death.

Digging with their hind legs, the dogs, the cats,
The cows, the rats and the others help her to fill up the ditch.
The striking of a bottle on a shovel serves as a death knell.
"Lions and tigers are cruel, vile and vicious!"
Buzz the flies and the albatross to the tune of *Dies Irae*.[43]
Under her top hat, Columbia looks like a real
Undertaker. "Kneel down! Pray!"
They're still praying. Will it be over soon? Whew! Finally, it's
    over!

172

A pack of zebras is marching to meet them.
How admirable. Their stripes are so beautiful, really!
Columbia hasn't enough limbs and contralto shouts
To hold back the tiger and the lion, enemies of fasting.

"I love those zebras! Have you understood? Love 'em like crazy!
I forbid you to go out carelessly to eat one or two of them!"
Big cats are strong. As if she were a casserole dish,
They send her rolling on the ground for the length of a league.

Everyone sits down. Time to watch the tiger and the lion do
    their thing.
Tails up, they leap right toward the zebras.
Everyone's ears are wide open. Everyone's eyes are open wide.
"To guess what happens next, you don't have to be an expert in
    algebra!"

Remarks Johann Sebastian Cur, foreseeing the worst.
But the big cats, instead of eating their fill, start to yap
(No one sees clearly what they're up to),
To bark just like sheep dogs.

By the sweat of their brows, without killing one, the tiger and
    the lion

Succeed in bringing the zebras to where Columbia and the
     others are.
The cows come to see what they smell like.
These pajama-wearing mules will quickly become their
     relatives.

173

For several reasons, the zebras come at a good time.
All zebra packs are overflown by flocks of vultures.
The albatross is suffering from being the only truly flying
     animal here.
It doesn't take him long to court the scavengers.

The vultures and the albatross speak the same language:
That of birds made to fraternize.
And their feathers aren't the same color.
(If you don't leave a message, you're screwed.)

He presents his buddies to Columbia and to the others.
On the ground, walking with their wings spread, the vultures seem
Like the police officers with ample black capes from Manna and
     Wother.
One of the vultures has a serpent-eater for a friend.

"How do you go about eating cobras without getting bitten?"
As interesting questions go, it's not so great.
But the interlocutor is nice, and won't make trouble.
"It's simple; I catch them by the tail."

The albatross talks to our poor Columbia about the
     serpent-eater.
Columbia is fascinated. "How brave serpent-eaters are!"
Columbia fears snakes as a sinner fears hell.
They reach the edge of the Red Sea under a cloudy sky.

174

They all swim across the Red Sea,
Including the vultures, the albatross and the serpent-eater.
You've got to follow the crowd if you want to be cool.
When I put salt in my tea, my table companions laugh.

You don't swim as well with talons as with webbed feet.
On the opposite bank, a plane full of people is waiting for them.
They wish to speak to our poor Columbia.
The rats and the others are not pleased.

"If you don't want to get bitten,
We suggest that you treat her right!"
"Miss Columbus? Well! What a mess!
Can't you move away a bit from this bestiary?"

"What's the matter? What's the big idea?"
Their leader, a historian, presents the problem to her.
"Canada has set up an extravagant festival
In order to celebrate your father's millennium. We love him!

As for you, you adored him. That's why you will agree
To come with us to give a little speech in Montreal
During the closing banquet. Follow us. Get on!"
"With them!" "Our air-and-sea plane is not big enough."

"Who cares. Go get another bigger one!"
Columbia's firmness makes her friends giggle.
"We'll be back. Wait for us. Don't move, my child!
We're coming back right away, Thursday at the latest."

175

Johann Sebastian Cur speaks up pompously.
"Columbia, we won't go with you in that airplane.
We'll use your absence to do something crazy."

"You're coming! And I'm the one in charge here, you little
    rascal!"

Everybody else gets involved. They don't want to go.
What's all this? What's gotten into them?
They have something wild to do in secret.
They're absolutely determined. Her cries leave them indifferent.

"I'll be gone for months. Where will you wait for me?"
Her eyes are brimming with tears, her heart is heavy as a house.
"Letting me leave alone, all alone. You're crazy!"
They need all the help they can muster. But she is right;

They can't let her leave alone, all alone.
She'll go with the ants that come from Canada.
What are they up to? Their faces are quite odd...
And where will they wait for her? Toward the west, in the Sahara.

"In the Sahara? It's big!" "It's a small world!"
They reply, mysteriously. The bigger plane is here!
Columbia boards it walking backwards, followed by the million
    ants
Designated to guard her body and the rest.

She can't wait to come back! She's frightened!
Suppose each one of them were to go back home!
She worries more than the roar of the motor
Of the air-and-sea plane, an aircraft bigger than the Trojan horse.

176

In her hotel room, she frets.
There's always someone who's after her.
There's the one who fills her hollow teeth with lead.
"You owe it to yourself to be healthy and beautiful."

There's the one who comes to wash her hair: an Italian.
There's the one who comes to take her temperature every morning.
There's the one who comes to brush her hair: a rascal.
There's the one who comes to teach her Greek and Latin.

"They sure have an effect on a crowd, sentences in those lingos.
Ite missa est. Oderint, dum metuant!"[44]
There's the one who came to measure her tits.
"Breasts are made for wearing a bra, my child."
There's the one who designs a Ricci dress for her
And who comes every other minute to have her try it on.
"Let me fix this... Let me fix that..."
There's the fuming perfumer. "Young lady, you smell of manure!"

"Go per-fumigate yourself!"
There's the one to whom she must tell her life story.
"Describe to me the first peenie you ever loved.
Tell me: for you, is the desire

To make love as strong
As the one to pee? Would you masturbate me?"
There's the one who tells her to be careful of her aorta.
There's no one who is even a bit sweet.

177

The historian in charge looks her over, explores her, feels her.
"Show me your teeth. Let me see your nails, your skirt."
He renders a favorable judgment. He judges her favorably.
She doesn't smell of manure anymore. Her little breasts, almost
      round,

Are solidly harnessed under her red dress which flows nicely.
Her teeth are as white as a sink, her nails pink.
He declares her ready to receive the representatives of the citizens,
The gentleman journalists, those who write in prose

Because some so-called silent partners don't like verse.
The ants have been locked into the bathroom.
"Stand up straight, my child! You're going to be in the newspapers.
Give'em hell!" "I'm all ready!"
She answers their silly questions sincerely.
"You slept in the same bed he did. What were his vices?"
"My father was a big fish eater.
He was flat broke. So he wasn't able to know greed."

"Did his nighttime habits make much noise?"
"The fish made him burp a lot, even in his sleep."
"What more intimate things do you know about him?"
"He had a weakness for red sturgeon."

"Give us some dirt, already! Say something! Talk to us!
Little girls, for example! Did he hand out caramels to them?
Did he like to finger soft things?
When you got on board, did he stay under the ladder?"

178

Assembled under the door, the ants don't miss a thing.
"Pull up your dress so we can glimpse your thighs!
Spread your legs! Puff out your tits! Smile!"
All around her, photographers scurry. They are jaundiced.

It's not necessary to be jaundiced in order to scurry.
Jaundice – you've guessed it – has nothing to do with this.
The ants don't like these nosy guys. Watching them flash
Lightning bolts, like Jupiter, they fear for their mama.

"You're just not sexy enough! Do I have to spell it out for you?"
They shout as though they wanted to hurt her.
"Good God! Give us some thigh! Something slutty!
What the hell is she, some kind of mental retard?"
If the ants get angry, the photographers are going to get theirs!

When a million ants let go to their heart's content, it gets ugly!
"All you have to do is tell me what to do in a calm voice."
"Go ask your mommy to heat up your milk."

That's the last straw. The bathroom door clicks.
As much flying as running, the ants throw themselves on them.
They cover them up with their movement as if with a sack.
They coat each one from head to toe.

Then they gnaw. They eat away at their clothes.
They eat into their skin, right down to the bone.
They even eat up, in no time at all,
The photographic equipment and the keys to their cars.

179

In the depressing market streets of Montreal,
It's snowing; the weather is cold enough to freeze the blood in
      your veins.
The ants don't give a darn about the cold. It's all the same to them.
They are exultant in their godmother's bra.

I hear the saintly hypocrites shout at the top of their lungs: "Help!"
Her sight is bad; her glasses are iced up.
The ants couldn't care less about the cold. Columbia has a
      heavy heart.
She can't see a blessed thing, not even a cat. She's really out of
      sorts.

In the streets, there's nothing but automobiles.
She looks under entrance steps. She looks in the back of
      courtyards.
She can't find a single cat. What a sad place this city is!
Behind her, a Chinese cat-hunter zigzags, runs.

She waits for him. Better to talk to a Chinese man than to a car.

He tells her his life story, why he hunts cats.
With those that he catches, he makes Chinese dishes, chow cat.
"I don't know what's happening; I don't understand.

No more than two days ago, there were lots of cats
Prowling in the streets and alleys of Montreal.
Yesterday, no pussycats, today not a single puss."
He cries like a newly orphaned child. He is dirty.

"I must have enough new competitors to fill up an auditorium."
Columbia takes the Chinese man in her arms, says sweet
        nothings to him.
A Chinese man needs affection just like an animal.
She talks softly to him and puts him on her lap.

180

The metropolis is sweating bullets, going nuts.
The S.P.C.A., the zoo and the city pound
Have just been savagely ravished.
Everything's been taken: mice, owls, bears, jackals.

All the animals in the number two Francophone city have been
        kidnapped.
That's not normal. That's not an everyday occurrence.
The coachmen on the Mount have had their horses stolen.
There aren't any more lice left in the hair of Montreal.

In the restrooms, not a cockroach is left.
I'm in the process of ruining this beautiful story.
Give me my coffin and I'll be gone. It's late.
It's quarter till midnight. There was one anteater,

Just one of them. He's gone, flown away.
The slaughterhouses on Frontenac Street have been ransacked.
Blay, clay, dlay, flay, glay, klay, mlay, nlay, play, rlay, slay;

Back, cack, dack, fack, gack, hack, jack, kack, lack, mack, nack,
     pack, rack.

There are many words that have no sense,
Monosyllables that are easily pronounceable but not in use.
My story would be much more in line with what I meant
If I could replace that PRONOUNCEABLE with a MLAY.

181

A sculptor has composed what Columbia must read.
Now, this artist is also a pornographer.
And he's made a mistake. How? I'm about to tell you.
Instead of giving the rover a ten-paragraph speech,

He has given her the first two chapters of his latest novel.
Dressed up and as sweet-smelling as a queen, as dazzling as the
     sun,
Standing tall in the footlights, she takes off her gloves.
The microphone, gold-plated, is a wonder.

"Alone, lying down on the northwest corner of Baffin's Island,
The handsome young man smokes, thinking sadly of Mary,
Of her long hair, above all of her big breasts.
Suddenly, he turns around: he has heard a shout.

It's she, rowing, bouncing all over the place!
She lands, just like C. Columbus at Santo Domingo."
The spongers at the closing banquet applaud.
They're relieved! Finally, a reference!

What the hell do they eat at a closing banquet?
Something to make the closing bank wet, but I'm not sure.
"He would eat her big eyes, black as ripe berries,
Just as a vegetarian eats greens.
He smiles at her. She falls into his arms.

She takes off her hat, her dress, her sandals, her stockings.
She takes her sweet time. He's glad about that.
So when will she take off her garter belt?"

182

It has become too dirty. Believing themselves to be victims by
     design,
The spongers take matters into their own hands.
They throw anything they can get their hands on at Columbia:
Sugar bowls, knives, salt shakers, toothpick holders.

Nothing is left on the tables of these nasty ones.
They take off their clothes and throw them at her.
Assembled in the prompter's box, the ants show their teeth.
They're waiting for the last straw. They rush out.

Guess the rest. I'm just too tired.
I'm going to take a little break from this silly work.
I'm like an airplane. Literary heights are right for me.
What is your favorite bread, madam? Pimperknuckle.

I can't wait to be done telling you this beautiful story.
When I'm all done, I'll exclaim, "Finally!"
Business will be good for some whore that night.
But I'd have to go without food and I'm hungry.

I can never say it enough: my existence sickens me.
I wish I could die without noticing. My poor mother!
She would go crazy if I killed myself. I'm not completely heartless.
My life has turned to vinegar. I'm as bitter as can be.

183

With the money found on the corpses at the closing banquet,
Columbia buys an airplane ticket.

What happened at the closing banquet truly grieves her.
"Ne marchez pas sur le gazon!" "Keep off the grass!"

Columbia walks on the grass while waiting for her airplane.
I'm sure that she would not walk on the grass
If she knew the French and English tongues,
The words of Paris and London.

She'd walk on the pavement like everyone else.
When you're not sick of everything, you're nice, obedient.
To be sick of everything is to want to shout: "Assholes!"
The plane for the Sahara is late from time to time.

She moves out of the way to let by a human being who
Is walking in the opposite direction on the same path as she.
She sees a human being of the female sex carrying a lemur cage.
It's empty. "What happened to your lemur?" she asks her.

"My lover, you say?" "Not your lover, your lemur..."
The pet worshipper throws herself into Columbia's arms.
"They stole it from me! Some animals stole it from me, my friend!
As for my poor lover, he's asleep, in a large tomb."

Columbia consoles the lady as best she can.
She coddles her like the child of one of her female dogs.
She pecks her cheek affectionately. She wipes her tears.
She gets slapped really hard. "*Vade retro,*[45] you dirty lesbian!"

184

Congratulating herself for having made friends among the animals,
Columbia climbs the moveable stairway of her plane.
She figures that if that lady had had a hammer,
She would have hit her with it right on the forehead.

The plane lands in Cairo. Cairo is hardly the Sahara.

The guy who sold her the ticket took her for a ride.
What to do, my God? She shall walk to the Sahara.
The Canadian ants follow as if it were a party.

They're not walking anymore. They've taken to their heels.
They're running. They can't wait to get back to Pauline-Émilienne,
Shalac, Bic, Johann Sebastian Cur, Badger, Sweetie-Pie.
I'll take advantage of this opportunity to tell you that the
     Canadian ants

Speak the same language as the Turkish, English and Spanish ones.
(Don't forget the silent partners! What do you expect?)
One ant, suddenly, loses consciousness. She has the measles.
They stop. Columbia hugs her, treats her, bandages her.

"Where did you catch these measles, my darling?" she asks.
"I don't know. Keep going nonetheless. Go on without me."
"You're not able to travel? Neither are we, my lovely.
We'll wait until your cured. Even if it takes a month!"

They arrive, long after, at the edge of the Sahara desert.
What she sees nearly kills her.
The last time that she saw it, that desert was empty and flat.
Now, it's hollow and full to the brim.

185

It is hollow like the sea and full of animals.
It is deeper than the Indian and Pacific Oceans,
And there are more animals than there is balderdash in the
     newspapers,
Than there is water in the China Sea and the Gulf of Mexico.

Something has happened, or else it's a dream.
Columbia finds Johann Sebastian Cur in the first row.
"Explain this to me. What have you done? What happened?

Where do these lemurs, camels, elephants come from?"

"Bic spoke of your gentleness to the lion who is king of all the
     animals.
He offers you his crown. Look at your subjects all looking at you,
With the exception of the fish and the mites. Isn't it beautiful?
Aren't you glad? Aren't you surprised? You're coughing?"

She's coughing indeed. She's caught a nasty cold.
"Why has the desert gotten so doggone deep?"
"It hollowed itself out under our teeth. Eat we would.
It was lowered because we haven't stopped eating its sand.

And if this continues, it won't be enough.
It's really time for us to get back on the road.
What else did you want us to make our meals with?
You had to come back quickly at all costs!

The desert is almost empty: we would have died of hunger!
Oh! Let's leave for a place with grass!"
She tells him to calm down, that they will leave tomorrow.
"Let's go right away or we will all become caustic!"

186

Standing on the head of the long-eared king of the elephants,
Cur lying at her feet, under a sky black with her birds,
Columbia leads the march to nowhere, the parade without equal.
She is happy: every pore of her skin exudes joy.

The lice are the smallest. They walk just behind her.
The giraffes walk at the rear. The tired swallows
Hold onto the eagles. The kiwi birds are wingless:
The vultures have started towing them in order to make them
     forget it.

Human beings without arms get drunk to forget...
They cross the Red Sea. They don't swim across it.
They were so thirsty that they drank it. They go through on foot.
Like the Hebrews, they reach the other shore dry.

They walk eastward, always eastward,
Between north and south, between the end of the world and the
    end of the world.
They all must advance at the same speed.
That makes the tortoises a bit furious.

187

The King of Arabia and his band block their way.
"Pillagers! You're going to lay waste the crops and the harvest!"
"Sir," utters Columbia, "we shall devastate nothing.
We shall pass through like the breeze. You shall feel a shiver:

What one feels going over a manhole."
The king of the lions, Amircal,[46] looks on with a disenchanted
    expression.
"What is the King of Arabia next to the Queen of us all?
Don't go down on your knees before these guys who are behind
    the times!"

Columbia, reddening for having trembled a little,
Brings out her voice for the days when she feels haughty.
"Sir, my friends are hungry. If they want to,
They'll eat your rice, your oats, your wheat. May it be known: I
    am the Queen

Of all the animals of the earth except the fish.
If your subjects are stronger than mine, crush us.
They are weaker. And by far. We would just
Gobble them up. And they would be quite tasty.

For we are hungry, as I told you before."
"Young lady, I shall complain at the first opportunity."
The animals' tears of laughter drown their sweat.
A mischievous porcupine approaches the king, and rubs itself
    against him.
"Ow!" The king's son kills the jokester with a blow of his sword.
In a trembling voice, Columbia shouts: "This means war!"
With great ceremony, sadly, the porcupine is buried.
As a down payment, the prince gets a hundred kicks in the butt.

188

The King of Arabia is thinking intensely about what just happened.
He won't complain to the You Enn. No! No way! Never!
"What?" it would say to him, "a few animals make you tremble?"
The You Enn doesn't know what they represent, doesn't know
    about

All the animals of the earth except the fish.
Its ignorance would lead it to laugh at a king in front of everyone.
The You Enn doesn't know that Columbia speaks to them and
    answers them.
The You Enn wasn't there a while ago. At the instant

When the porcupine expired, the eyes of the elephants, the
    sparrowhawks
And all the others seemed charged with electricity.
They would have devoured him there if they had not been held
    back.
That girl Columbia told them: "The moment has not come."

They draw up a peace treaty. "Welcome to the animals!"
They can eat whatever they want, as much as they're able.
Everywhere on his lands they shall have something to drink. If
    necessary,
Young lady, my subjects will sing as you pass.

The King of Arabia is laughing up his sleeve.
Without his diplomacy, his people would almost all be eaten up.
He shouts: "Allah, I just saved my country!"
Tomorrow at dawn, he'll have a one-thousand-foot statue of
    himself erected.

189

The little Arabs, the children, throw kisses at Columbia.
They've been trained. They do what they're told.
The big Arabs, the adults, really want to throw bombs at her.
They seem, if you like, to hate her all to hell.

They gaze at her with a look that says: "Go away!"
The Arabs are just as hopeless as the Mannese.
Tigers and lions look at the Arabs, little and big, avidly.
After dining on sand and on wheat, they're losing fur, losing
    weight.

On this diet, the black panthers have become white.
As for the dung-beetles, they have no complaints to make.
The cows of the Far West tell each other ranch stories.
For the ticks, sand and wheat are also last resorts.

Having entered this kingdom in the month of May,
They leave it in the month of November, in the rain.
The herbivores are fat, sated with the grasses.
The carnivores still feel hungry.

190

Five hundred carnivores are gravely ill.
Columbia hugs them and bandages them with love.
It doesn't help. The king of the lions, pale and staggering,
Withdraws with Columbia to the top of a tower.

"Let us reflect!" she says to him, completely desperate.
She reflects intensely. Amircal reflects deeply.
No way to make vegetarians out of carnivores.
That's clear. They've tried their best and they're half dead.

How can one get flesh and blood
When one does not wish to have recourse to methods so criminal?
Columbia feels a crushing burden upon her shoulders.
She'd find a solution if she were more intellectual.

The end! All that's left to do is to go jump in a lake.
"What about human beings?" hurls Amircal, as if with a gun.
"They don't think twice before gorging themselves on beef flesh!
They even boast when they've eaten a good roast!

They've made a sport out of torturing the fish!
All our problems are solved: just say the word."
There is great wisdom in the lion's words.
Hemingway! Cowboys! Safaris! Gourmet cooks! The bastards!

191

In Asia, there's not much of anything good for carnivores.
There are the pashas, their gangs, the chic tourists.
That's all. The rest are as thin as a sheet of paper.
In Asia, they're not clever like in America:

They are nothing more than skin and bones.
Columbia has led the most gravely ill
Into the palace harem of the pasha of Kazo.
To get your color back, what better than carousing women!

"Big beautiful thighs! And those rumps!" recounts a tiger.
"You had to be hungry: there are no words for it.
I had fasted for eight months! It was delicious. Gosh!
You should have seen us! You should have been there!"

192

A meeting of the most powerful humans is held in New York.
The carnivores are the talk of the whole world.
The newspapers are making quite a racket about their carnage.
They just ate one hundred thousand servicemen in China.

The most powerful humans try to come up with an agreement.
"The animals have polished off the Chinese army in next to no
    time.
This is alarming! Aren't humans strong enough?
They'll eat your son Frank; they'll gnaw away at your daughter
    Frances!"

The powerful human who just spoke is eloquent.
That familiar way he has! He's surely an American!
A general speaks up. He has a plan. He's from France.
"Gentlemen, my plan is simple. I came up with it yesterday
    morning."

The French general's plan is chosen by acclamation.
They will let them advance to the middle of the Gobi desert.
When they get that far, helicopters and airplanes
Will be able – without killing humans, a forbidden act –

To shower them with atomic bombs and hydrogen bombs.
"Gentlemen, the meeting of the most important humans has ended.
The French general's plan is adopted." The president, curtly,
Has just adjourned the meeting. The assassins will be assassinated.

193

The storks are quite flattered and quite surprised
To hear Columbia speak their language fluently.
"My dear, where did you learn to speak our beautiful tongue?"
Taking the storks by the neck, all the while savoring a mango,

Poor Columbia tells them the wonderful story of the friendship
That she had with the stork who, long ago, used to sleep
Standing up on the mast of the bottomless yacht. They listen to her.
It's as if it were Homer recounting the tale.

"But she was old. She died of a fever in Bulgaria."
The storks seek family ties to the one
Who was the queen's first friend. "A stork from Russia...
I myself am from that country. May we know to which

Family she belonged? Did she have blue eyes like mine?"
Columbia responds as well as she can to their questions.
"Only the Vainenfake sleep standing up on a mast.
I myself am Vainenfake. I'm so moved!"

"You've got another thing coming. I'm not Vainenfake
And, to this day, whenever I could, I've slept standing up on a
    mast."
"I knew a Vainenfake. In Peru, she was my neighbor:
She slept in a ditch just like me."

"If you're the husband of a Vainenfake, she sleeps where you
    sleep."
"I wasn't her husband. How dare you! What business is it of yours!
What's more, the Vainenfake, if you want to know, are too
    ferocious
And too ugly for me. I like the sweet and lovely ones!"

194

They are in the middle of the magnificent Gobi desert.
Helicopters and airplanes shower them with bombs,
Atomic and hydrogen bombs "made in the USA."
Dying by the thousands, they think only of Columbia's safety.

Under the power of the explosives, elephant trunks, giraffe

Necks, vulture beaks and cock crests swirl around.
Columbia has not moved. She has remained on her elephant,
     standing up.
"Come on, Columbia! Hurry up!" shouts a giant tortoise, all
     agitated.

"Columbia, go into the shell of that giant tortoise!"
Being torn to shreds by the thousands, the animals beg their queen
To hide, to take shelter. She does not agree.
She wants to aid the wounded. "It's not worth it!"

Getting angry, a gorilla hides Columbia with his powerful arms.
"Think of your post! What would become of us, without you?"
Columbia sticks her head out of the shell. The blue sky is blood
     red.
Sliced into pieces, their heads, feet, and tails drown in it.

The poor queen loses consciousness. Relieved, the tortoise
Pulls her crown and her head under its carapace.
Unless a bomb falls right on top,
This giant tortoise will save her life. This giant tortoise is made

To last through the most violent atomic wars.
By thousands upon thousands, the animals have been killed.
By the millions, the animals continue to be killed. Without panic,
The animals wait for it to be over, for it to be done.

195

With an enormous bulldozer, Columbia digs an immense ditch.
With an enormous sequoia, Columbia builds an immense cross.
As you suspect, they are not exactly enjoying themselves.
They are sad. They are deadly sad. They don't have a choice.

"It's them, or it's us!" Amircal, king of the lions,
Doesn't mince his words. They decide to kill all of the humans.

"Despite our losses, we remain more numerous than they.
Suppose we attack tonight. They'll all be dead tomorrow."

These proud words give goose pimples to everyone.
Amircal, Bic, Cur and Columbia are meeting behind closed doors.
They're making plans. Bic is the one who is the most loquacious.
She says they mustn't commit sins of presumption. The weather
    is gorgeous.

The sun shines intensely. "I've heard," says the ant,
"That certain tortoises speak the language of the water animals.
The fish are tired of getting eaten. That's for sure. Really!
Just look at them! There are many of us. That's true. But not too
    many.

There could never be too many of us." She is silent, giving
Her words time to produce their effect. "And the bacteria?
Nothing is more murderous than those germs! They're hardly
    reassuring!
And I know some ticks who know some anaerobes..."

The meeting now over, a delegation is sent to the king of the fish.
A deputation is sent to the germs and the bacteria.
Armed with oxygen masks and chair legs, the fish will be able
To walk without difficulty on land and breathe the air. So it is.

196

Through a great telescope, Al Capone watches the animals
Do their thing, laughing. He laughs, as you suspect, because he
    is glad.
If this keeps up, he won't have enough bordellos and
Gambling houses. If this keeps up, paradise won't be big enough.

The more humans die, the more clients Al Capone has. It's
Easy to understand. The fifty-two thousand doors of heaven

Are open. The poor ticket collectors don't even have time
To sleep. The states of venial sin and the states of mortal sin

Are crowding the doors. The animal forces have two fronts.
The fish and the birds take charge of one side of the Atlantic,
And the others of the other side. World War II didn't do any better.
The snakes bite them. The elephants knock them senseless. The
     bloodsuckers

Make the blood gush forth. Al Capone laughs, showing his
     thirty teeth of gold.
"Will you look at those fish! Oxygen masks! Chair legs!
Just too funny! Just too funny!" The more he laughs, the hotter
     he gets.
Al Capone orders Saint Peter to turn down all the furnaces.

What is that ant doing? She's going into the mouth of a man
     from Nice,
Slipping into his esophagus, reaching his heart, stopping it.
A single ant can knock out a hundred enemies quite easily.
That takes the wind out of your sails, huh? For whoever has the
     heart,

Killing is easy. As for Columbia Columbus, she cries and does not
Intervene. How can she tell the fish not to kill kids,
She who as a kid killed so many fish? She cries a lot.
One more hour, and they'll all be dead: men, women and children.

Notes

1   Albéric Cahuet was a seldom recognized yet prolific French novelist. "Jehan Ethiey-Blez" evokes the eminent 20th-century Quebecois literary critic, Jean Éthier-Blais, who has often been highly critical of Réjean Ducharme's works. (Translator's note.)

2   Pierre Corneille, the French dramatic poet (1606-1684), was the principal creator of neoclassical theater in France. (Translator's note.)

3   Manon Lescaut is the insatiable young woman in *Manon Lescaut*, by French novelist Abbé Prévost (1697-1763). (Translator's note.)

4   "Tricholome" is a fairly big, fleshy mushroom of the agaric family with jagged gills – not a fish. The word is from the Greek, "tricho" + "loma," or "hairy fringe." Perhaps it is not a coincidence that the term in French also suggests "triche-Colombe," to "cheat" or "trick" Columbia. In any case, she is indeed tricked by this poisonous fish-mushroom. (Translator's note.)

5   This question is written in English in the original French text: "How much does it cost?". (Translator's note.)

6   The original French phrase, "Rufi sur l'onde" ("Rufi on the wave") plays on the somewhat old-fashioned expression "payer rubis sur l'ongle" (literally, "to pay rubies on the [finger]nail"). In English, the equivalent expression is "to pay cash on the nail"; hence, the play on words may be rendered as "cash on the fingernail." (Translator's note.)

7   Dagobert is the absent-minded king who is the subject of a well-known nursery rhyme: "Le bon roi Dagobert avait ses culottes à l'envers . . ." (Good King Dagobert wore his trousers inside out . . . "). (Translator's note.)

8   The original French novel is written in verse, mostly in the rhyme scheme of *abab*, and degenerates into prose toward the end of the text. The narrator sometimes (sardonically) goes to great lengths to preserve the rhyme at the end of a quatrain, even risking a non sequitur such as this line. (Translator's note.)

9   In his frustration, the narrator apparently resorts to ersatz Latin. (Translator's note.)

10   "Better watch your Perse!" is meant to approximate the original "Des vrais petits Saint-Léger Léger!", which is a reference to Alexis Saint-Léger Léger (1887-1975), the French diplomat and poet whose pseudonym was St. John Perse. In French, to take something lightly, "au

léger," is the opposite of taking it seriously, "au sérieux," as in the previous line. (Translator's note.)

11   The adjective "curule" refers to those of the highest rank: only the most privileged civil officers of Rome could sit on the "curule chair." The play on words here is between "curule fate" and "cruel fate." (Translator's note.)

12   This sentence appears to be another non sequitur whose purpose is to maintain the rhyme scheme in the original text. (Translator's note.)

13   *La Franciade*, translated here as a "Gallic epic," was an unfinished attempt (1574) by the French poet Pierre de Ronsard (1524-1585) to write an epic history of the founding of the kingdom of France. The implication here is that Ducharme is proposing his own fictive version of the founding of America. (Translator's note.)

14   "Khedive" was the title of the Turkish viceroys of Egypt, 1867-1914. (Translator's note.)

15   Hey, that's very pretty. (Editor's note.)

16   My intent is to be outstanding in the field of foolishness. (Author's note.)

17   Potassium nitrate. (Translator's note.)

18   In the original text, the expletives are derived from objects used in the Catholic liturgy; they form a key part of the working-class slang in Quebec known as "joual." (Translator's note.)

19   A French popular singer. (Translator's note.)

20   Thurifer: in liturgical rites, the acolyte or altar boy who carries the thurible, which contains incense. Figuratively, a flatterer or syco-phant. (Translator's note.)

21   That doesn't exist. (Author's note.)

22   The preceding canto seems to be very reactionary. Those who have considered me *engagé* are going to be glad. (Author's note.)

23   Big fucks. (Author's note.)
       N.B. In the original, "chef de gare" (stationmaster) plays on "chef d'œuvre" (masterpiece). I have similarly deformed "masterpiece" into "masterpiss." Moreover, Ducharme's footnote plays on "cossus" (well-to-do) and "cocus" (cuckolded). I have rendered the pair as "big bucks" and "big fucks." (Translator's note.)

24   The purposeful use of "parce que" is faithful to the author's incon-spicuous placement of the English word "because" in the original French text. (Translator's note.)

25   St. Evarist was Pope around 97 A.D. (Translator's note.)

26   By analogy with ashtray. (Author's note.)

27   At first, in chapter XVIII, the priest is presented as Joanna's brother. Here, he is identified as one of her two sons, i.e., as the brother of Paul Blablabla. (Translator's note.)

28   Charles Fourier (1772-1837), a French socialist philosopher. (Translator's note.)

29   "Pauline-Émilienne" may refer to Paul-Émile, Cardinal Léger, the former archbishop of Montreal. See also the brief appearance of Paul-Émile Ropre in Chapter XXXV. (Translator's note.)

30   Black. (Author's note.)

31   Chandernagor: a city in India, a former French settlement. (Translator's note.)

32   A Greek popular singer who sings in French, Greek, Spanish and several other languages. She is known for her thin, dark-rimmed, rectangular glasses. (Translator's note.)

33   It's a rhinoceros with forty horns. (Author's note.)

34   Randall Jarrell's 1963 poem "Next Day" opens with a similar pun on brand names of soaps and detergents: "Moving from Cheer to Joy, from Joy to All, / I take a box / And add it to my wild rice, my Cornish game hens." (Translator's note.)

35   Omphale, in Greek mythology, was a queen of Lydia who married Hercules, but only after he had dressed as a woman and done womanly chores for her for three years, in order to appease the gods. (Translator's note.)

36   Álvaro Obregón was president of Mexico (1920-1924) and was noted for his anticlericalism. After being re-elected, he was assassinated in 1928. (Translator's note.)

37   Offspring of a goose. (Author's note.)

38   A Czech composer. (Translator's note.)

39   A Finnish composer. (Translator's note.)

40   U.O.I.L.S.A.T.O.

41   U.T.S.

42   The reference is to the poem "L'Albatros" ("The Albatross"), by French poet Charles Baudelaire (1821-67). (Translator's note.)

43   "Day of anger," the title and first words of one of the five Latin hymns sung in the Roman Catholic funeral Mass. (Translator's note.)

44   "The Mass is ended; go (in peace). Let them hate me, as long as they fear me!" (Translator's note.)

45   "Get thee behind me." (Translator's note.)

46   "Amircal," in addition to evoking Admiral ("Amiral" in French), is "Lacrima," or "Tears," spelled backward in Latin. (Translator's note.)

Afterword

The Daughter of Christopher Columbus, an iconoclastic novel masquerading as an epic poem, is the fourth of Réjean Ducharme's nine novels to date. Written in the mid-1960s and published by Éditions Gallimard in Paris in 1969, it is an ambitious fictive rewriting of the encounter between Europe and the Americas in light of the modern demythification of Columbus. It portrays the adolescence and young adulthood of Columbia Columbus, an imaginary daughter of the explorer, mysteriously "born of the famous egg of her notorious father" in the middle of the twentieth century (ch. 4). Virulent misogyny, rampant racism and sexism, the virgin/whore complex, raging automobiles, an acerbic critique of academic life, a devastating portrait of the corrupt communications media, and a relentless attack on the tyranny of labor unions are but some of the highlights of the textual terrain. Such intense dissatisfaction with life is within the tradition of Quebec's Quiet Revolution *(la Révolution tranquille)* of the 1960s, which attacked the *status quo* in language, literature, social relationships, politics and religion. Indeed, the biting anti-clericalism of the narration reflects a Franco-Canadian society that for centuries had been both sustained and stifled by the Catholic Church, with all of its structures and strictures. The challenge for the translator of this novel in verse is to take a rhymed text in poetic form – one whose frequently tortured verse is unraveling before our very eyes – and transform it into English prose in the shape of an epic poem, guarding all the while the contumacious, cantankerous spirit of the French original.

This is a coming-of-age novel in which the protagonist is Ducharme's vehicle for a rollicking chronicle of the contradictions and scandals of his own era. In this tale of woe, virtually everything that can possibly happen to Columbia does: rape, pillage, betrayal, murder, dismemberment, and so forth. Of course, she always comes back for more. Having inadvertently poisoned her father, Columbia discovers that true friends are few and far between, in this world where Al Capone has taken over heaven and earth and has designs on hell (ch. 72). Eventually, Columbia gives up on human beings and finds consolation among the animals, who welcome her and declare her Queen of the Animals. A new pied piper, she leads an ever-increasing number of animals of almost all species across North America, Africa and Asia, moving from west to east in an inversion of the east-west movement of Christopher Columbus's actual voyages. But this moveable feast, this traveling utopia, is destined to collide with certain biological realities: the carnivores must eat meat, unlike the herbivores. That imperative sews the seeds of the animals' inevitable and disastrous confrontation with human beings, who taste quite good to lions and tigers... The plot culminates in an apocalyptic nuclear war between humans and animals.

The Daughter of Christopher Columbus is far from politically correct, to say the least. It takes its place, however, in a politically correct cultural project: it joins the long line of works that have proposed the demythification of Columbus, such as *The Crown of Columbus* by Michael Dorris and Louise Erdrich, Carlos Fuentes's *Christopher Unborn*, and Georges-Hébert Germain's *Christophe Colomb, Naufrage sur les côtes du Paradis (Christopher Columbus, Foundering on the Coast of Paradise)*. Unlike these works, which were published just before the quincentennial of Columbus's "discovery" of America, Ducharme's novel in verse appeared in 1969, years before the scholarly and media hype about 1992. Moreover, Ducharme's new *Columbiad* dispenses promptly with Columbus the father and proceeds to a *re*-mythification of its own through the character of the daughter. In the novel, Columbia Columbus attends the celebration of an anniversary yet to come: magically, in the year 2492, she is flown to Montreal in the company of her Canadian ant bodyguards to mark the millennium of her father's exploits (ch. 174).

Most of Ducharme's novels have ambiguous, idiosyncratic titles that play on double meanings (e.g, *L'Océantume*, usually rendered as *Bittersea*). In *The Daughter of Christopher Columbus*, the enigma lies rather in the question of its literary genre, for the text is presented in the form of an epic which cannot contain the explosive content of a novel. Like a growing number of holes in a dike, the novel at first seeps and finally bursts through the traditional literary constraints of the genre of epic poetry. The confrontation between the human species, intelligent and arrogant, and the animal kingdom, untamed but standing in solidarity with Columbia, evolves parallel to the generic struggle within the text between the epic and the novel. All of this results in a novel epic subverted and liberated in a process known as *novelization*. It is a startling transformation of stanzas into a space of prosodic parody, even travesty. This novelization is apparent not only in the degeneration of the narrative, but also in the debasement of the poetic form into tortured verse and finally into prose, peppered all the while with the narrator's existential complaints and attacks on the reader. Novelization occurs even in the character and person of Columbia, through the hyperbolic, misogynistic dismemberment of her body at the hands of cruel profiteers. In these three ways – the degeneration of the narrative, the debasement of the poetic form, and the dismemberment of Columbia – *The Daughter of Christopher Columbus* is an archetype of the novelization of the epic that Bakhtin perceives on a larger scale in the evolution of world literature.

Ducharme's genius is in iconoclastic wordplay, in the constant disruption of the reader's expectations through the mixing of formal and informal registers, in the incongruous juxtaposition of the sacred and the profane. The narrator of *The Daughter of Christopher Columbus* sets several hurdles for the reader at the very start of the text. Far from welcoming the reader, the blatantly misogynistic preface seems to dare the reader to continue at her own risk. The tale itself begins in a roundabout, inaccessible way. The narrator's attitude seems to be: prove to me that you'll put up with me no matter what – show me unconditional reading – and only then will I tell you the whole story. Several strands of the text involve interruptions and digressions: novelization gradually breaks down the stanzas of the epic, in the end leaving nothing but streams of prose that happen to be in poetic form (ch. 196).

The narrator also interrupts himself, disrupting the thematic unity of the "beautiful story" of Columbia through his complaints of existential angst, depression and suicidal thoughts. An example of this *textus interruptus*, and a turning point in the telling of the tale, is the narrator's morose declaration in chapter 160 that his verse is getting worse and worse:

> If I were less nauseated by life,
> I would probably tell you this beautiful story better.
> When one feels like committing suicide, my dear,
> The verse gets worse and bursts as you go along.

This is followed immediately by another major excursus from the narration, the attack on strikers and labor unions (ch. 161 and 162), in which the narrator cites the strike of May 17, 1966, as a low point in his existence. In this diatribe, the predictable rhymed quatrains explode into stanzas of five, seven or eight lines, sometimes with no attempt at rhyme whatsoever. This is Ducharme's textual declaration of war on the epic poem, a literary disruption parallel to the upcoming atomic war between the humans and the animals, the ultimate interruption of Columbia's wanderings. War, in both the struggle over genre in the text and the evolution of the plot, disrupts the cosmic peace on every level. *The Daughter of Christopher Columbus* is a battlefield between the classic epic form and the chaotic modern novel, as well as a confrontation between supposedly "civilized" humans and "beastly" animals. The degeneration of the epic parallels Columbia's failure to find lasting human friendship in our stilted, mendacious, superficial society. Columbia's increasing alienation from humans and corresponding solidarity with animals parallels the increasingly chaotic novelization of the text.

This degeneration of the epic is reflected even in the number-ing of the chapters, through the degradation of the initial Roman numerals and the conflicting juxtaposition of Roman and Arabic symbols. After an unremarkable start, with chapters I, II, III, etc., the numbering spins out of control. Ever more absurd neo-Roman numerals appear in chapters 40 through 101: forty is rendered as XXXX, instead of the standard LX, and one hundred one as XXXXXXXXXXI, instead of the standard CI. Thus, as Colum-bia's desperate search for friendship among humans comes to a close in chapter one hundred and one, the Roman numerals reach the height of absurdity. Then, starting in chapter 102, Arabic nu-merals appear out of nowhere, symbolizing the beginning of her new life, a Christ-like search for animal disciples, and highlighting the shift from epic to novel. All this is presented by a narrator who shows no little or no respect for the reader. In a series of passive-aggressive attacks on the reader, the narrator once again dares us to continue, flirts inelegantly with an implied female reader, and in general calls into question the entire enterprise through his sweep-ing nihilism.

Seek not the man behind the nihilistic text: Ducharme, who is among the foremost Quebecois writers of the twentieth century, has been a recluse for more than thirty years. Born in Saint Félix-de-Valois, Quebec, in 1941 or 1942 (his own ambiguity), he burst onto the literary scene on both sides of the Atlantic in 1966 with Gallimard's publication of the now-canonical *L'Avalée des avalés (The Swallower Swallowed)*. Ducharme has shunned any contact with the public or with its media representatives. In one of his only interviews, in 1966, Ducharme told poet and journalist Gérald Godin that he wanted his works to be known, but never his per-sonal life. Since the late 1960s, he has gone to great lengths to maintain his anonymity, outdoing even J. D. Salinger, the secretive author of *The Catcher in the Rye*. Under the pseudonym of Roch Plante, Ducharme has exhibited sculptures gleaned from trash re-trieved during his nocturnal walks in Montreal. He has collabo-rated as a songwriter with Quebecois singer Robert Charlebois; he has written film scenarios for Francis Mankiewics, including the riveting *Les Bons débarras* (*Good Riddance*, 1979); he has written several plays and a total of nine novels, the most recent of which are *Va Savoir* (*Go Figure*, 1994), and *Gros mots* (*Big Bad Words,* 1999). And yet, apart from *The Daughter of Christopher Columbus*, only one of the plays, two of the novels and an excerpt of a third have been translated into English. Why? Because his writing is highly creative and a challenge to the translator, and because Ducharme chooses not to play the media game.

Réjean Ducharme is a living symbol of the alienation of postmodern Western society. His writing shows us what we have become: twisted, rigid, obsessed, violent, mindless adults who have forgotten the beautiful world of our childhoods, when everything was still possible. Forewarned is forearmed: some writing is successful to the degree to which it makes many readers intensely uncomfortable, even as it thrills and amuses them. This is the charm of Ducharme. As Marie-Claire Blais wrote in 1969, when Ducharme was increasingly isolated: "Il faut une parole d'accueil" ("A Word of Welcome is in Order"). Writers of conscience are rare, even when full of their own contradictions. The texts of Ducharme? Never good riddance, always good reading.

Will Browning
Boise State University

Acknowledgments

I wish to express my gratitude to Antonio D'Alfonso of Guernica Editions, who has steadfastly believed in the importance of publishing Ducharme's writing in translation. Without the patient diplomacy and encouragement of Rolf Puls of Éditions Gallimard, this project would not have seen the light of day. My thanks to Jacques Cotnam and to Daniel Jourlait for their guidance in the early stages of this enterprise. And of course, I thank Claire Richard, Ducharme's representative, and Réjean Ducharme himself, for authorizing the publication of *The Daughter of Christopher Columbus*.

I offer my heartfelt appreciation to Teresa Boucher, Anaïse Boucher-Browning, and Renaud Boucher-Browning who have supported, tolerated and celebrated this undertaking in every way since its inception.

W.B.

Other Works by Réjean Ducharme
Available in English

"From *Bittersea* (novel)," excerpt translated by David Homel in *Exile* 7.1-2 (1980): 43-64. Originally *L'Océantume*. Paris: Gallimard, 1968.

Ha Ha!... (play). English translation by David Homel. Toronto: Exile, 1986. Originally *Ha ha!....* Paris: Gallimard, 1982; Saint Laurent, Quebec: Éditions Lacombe, 1982.

The Swallower Swallowed (novel). English translation by Barbara Bray. London: Hamish Hamilton, 1968. Originally *L'Avalée des avalés*. Paris: Gallimard, 1966; Montreal: Bélier, 1967; Collection Folio, Paris: Gallimard, 1982.

Wild to Mild (novel). English translation by Robert Guy Scully. Saint-Lambert, Quebec: Héritage, 1980. Excerpt translated as "The Zone of Hardy Deciduous Forests" by Ray Chamberlain in *Exile* 3.3-4 (1976): 66-114. Originally *L'Hiver de force*. Paris: Gallimard, 1973; Collection Folio, Paris: Gallimard, 1984.